TO
CHANGE A LIFE

LARRY BRADY

TO CHANGE A LIFE

PANAMA BOOK

TATE PUBLISHING
AND ENTERPRISES, LLC

To Change a Life
Copyright © 2013 by Larry Brady. All rights reserved.

No part of this publication may be reproduced, stored in a retrieval system or transmitted in any way by any means, electronic, mechanical, photocopy, recording or otherwise without the prior permission of the author except as provided by USA copyright law.

Scripture quotations, unless otherwise indicated, are taken from the Holy Bible, King James Version, Cambridge, 1769. Used by permission. All rights reserved.

Scripture quotations marked (asv) are taken from the American Standard Version, Thomas Nelson & Sons, 1901. Used by permission. All rights reserved.

The opinions expressed by the author are not necessarily those of Tate Publishing, LLC.

Published by Tate Publishing & Enterprises, LLC
127 E. Trade Center Terrace | Mustang, Oklahoma 73064 USA
1.888.361.9473 | www.tatepublishing.com

Tate Publishing is committed to excellence in the publishing industry. The company reflects the philosophy established by the founders, based on Psalm 68:11,
"The Lord gave the word and great was the company of those who published it."

Book design copyright © 2013 by Tate Publishing, LLC. All rights reserved.
Cover design by Ronnel Luspoc
Interior design by Jomar Ouano

Published in the United States of America

ISBN: 978-1-62510-934-7
1. Religion / Christian Life / Personal Growth
2. Religion / Christian Ministry / Missions
13.06.20

CONTENTS

Foreword 7
Introduction 11

To Change a Life 19
Building Relationships 25
It Is More Blessed to Give Than to Receive 37
To Fulfill a Command 41
You Buy My Sister 47
A Boy Who Lost a Dollar 53
Finding a Ministry 57
A Great and Effectual Door 61
This Man Is Dying 65
I Have Not Seen Such a Great Faith 69
My Name Is Danely 79
We Can Do That 85
The Blind See 93
Papa Larry Is Coming 97
Where There Is Hope There Is Life 107
A Distorted Picture 117
God Is Big 123
The Man with a Big Smile 131

Fulfilling a Promise 157
The Gift of Eggs 165
A Beautiful Smile 171
How Are You? 177
Alto de la Playon 181
A Wheelchair for Mother 187
Christmas on the Chucunaque River 193
Keeping the Mission Interesting 205
Snakes, Chiggers, and Picking Rice 217
I'm Not Driving Down That Cliff 221
The Clinic of Hope 227
What Pleases God 233
Finding Happiness 237
How Mission Work Changed Our Lives 241
The End of the Road 277

Conclusion 281

FOREWORD

Questions of purpose or calling or true vocation or the passion of the soul live in our consciousness all our lives. Generally dormant, at certain moments, they jump on to front stage. The high school senior, the recently widowed, the new college graduate, the demobilized soldier, the suddenly unemployed, the discontented worker, the restless retiree—these situations cause us to reflect on what is important in life and to what extent we are living a life of purpose that reflects our own rare and distinctive gifts. What was I put here to accomplish? If we believe, as I do, that each of us is especially and uniquely created, there must exist something special and unique that each is meant to do. Those who have truly wrestled with these questions and thus have come to the recognition of their own singular path are shining lights for the rest of us, giving us hope and energy for our own journeys.

Whenever I ponder these questions, my thoughts always come around to my friend Larry Brady. In early 2003, I was the newly arrived ambassador of the United States to Panama, giving much thought to the realigned relationship of our two countries now that the Canal was in Panamanian hands, forever changing the nature of our strategic partnership (and for the better, I might add). I realized that the best avenue for the United States was to express our respect for the people of Panama and to demonstrate how we, as a government, as businesses, as individuals, were extending a hand of friendship toward Panamanians. As I began to articulate this message, I was fortunate enough to run across a fellow named Larry Brady, who ran a program called Panama Missions. Nobody ever just "meets" Larry. It's more like getting sucked up into Larry's vortex or his energy field for lack of a better term, is so activated and magnetic that you just get drawn in by its power and force and you are never the same again.

Here is a man who, as a young soldier, was assigned to the Panama Canal Zone. He saw extreme poverty in Panama and decided that he would do something about it. I think it was more along the lines of him having to do something about it. He was not able not to do something about it. That is the calling, the vocation. Larry Brady, by the grace of God, stumbled upon the work that would give his life meaning, that would fulfill his purpose, that would take his unique talents and transform him and everyone who knows him. I'm not sure that Larry would call what he does in Panama work. I feel certain he would say it is his joy, his faith in action, his gift to others. It is his ministry. Being a minister, of course, is much more than preaching a sermon or teaching about God. It is living one's life in such a way as to bring life and hope to others. In Christianity, a minister sees Jesus in all people and love and cares for others as though they were Christ. That is why "All members are ministers," as some churches put it, is such a powerful message. All are called to minister, to be the hands of Christ in the world, to show the love of God to those in need. Tom Ford, a Panamanian who has spent his life helping others, is a close collaborator of Larry's. He was once asked how Larry was able to do what he does, so much for so many. Tom's answer—he looked up and pointed his finger at the heavens. His message was clear: this is a man whose help cometh from the Lord.

This book will have special meaning to all Christians who are striving to find purpose in their lives. But my hope is that it will be read by people across the religious and secular spectrum, by all who seek a greater sense of purpose to their lives, by all who seek inspiration for taking a leap of faith, by all who may have good intention but who doubt their own capabilities to make a difference. Larry's story has highs and lows, times of uncertainty and doubt, times when he didn't know if the money would suffice. But his is a story of triumph, of—above all—persistence, of powerful commitment.

I have been privileged to witness the results. For Panama, Larry's work keeps hopes alive in the remote Darién Province, usually forgotten and ignored by those with power and influence. Panama Missions is literally saving lives there. For the individuals reached by Panama Missions, the stories are countless, and you will read about many of them in this book. Students who might not even have learned to read well are going to high school and college and medical school. Children have received lifesaving surgeries. Dentists and optometrists and nutritionists have visited remote villages and treated people who have no access to health care. Children receive Christmas boxes lovingly and thoughtfully prepared every year by Larry's legions of supporters. Sick children get a visit from Santa. Sometimes though, I feel that the best gift Larry brings is *love*. I have seen the faces of poor Panamanian Indians who are absolutely marginalized and dismissed by their own government and society light up when Larry is around with his joy and spirit of generosity. And working with Panama Missions has transformed the lives of hundreds of Americans who volunteer their time and donate their money. To get caught up in Larry's vortex is to experience a sublime emotion that combines compassion, satisfaction, joy, strength, and, yes, the soul's passion. Reading this book will lift you up and inspire your own journey of life-giving purpose.

Linda E. Watt
US Ambassador to Panama, 2002–2005
Chief Operating Officer, The Episcopal Church, 2007–2011

INTRODUCTION

In July 1984 I traveled to The Republic Panama for the first time with the United States Air Force. The purpose of this trip was as an aircraft technician on the C-130 Hercules. I was not looking for a mission and had never given it a thought that one day I would become a missionary. This was the furthest thing from my mind. I had been a minister since I was 23 years old working in mostly small churches in South Alabama. I had no training in missionary work and never gave it a second thought. Wherever I traveled throughout the world if I was in a location over Sunday I always looked for a church where I could worship. We landed on Saturday and as soon as I had checked in I began making inquiries. I found the name of a member of the church of Christ in what is called the canal zone. The next day I was picked up by one of the members who gave me a ride to church. As most of the churches of all different faiths were composed of military families with a few Panamanians who were also English-speaking. The following Sunday I was asked if I would preach due to the preacher returning to the United States. I gladly accepted and was invited to return in November 1984 to speak in a revival. Even then I did not consider this as mission work but rather an opportunity to preach the gospel which I enjoyed doing. However this began a mission work that would span three decades and continues even today with hundreds of people traveling to Panama on mission trips with me each year. As you will read in this book tens of thousands of people throughout Panama have been the recipients of the compassion of godly men and women composed of doctors and nurses, dentists and surgeons who gave so freely of their talents. There were also contractors, engineers electricians, block layers, evangelist, teachers and many young people getting their first taste of mission work. What caused me to continue and what causes others to return over and over helping people they do not know? That is what this book is all about.

As I began to become aware of the poverty and of so many needs throughout Panama I began to read more about the ministry of Jesus paying particular attention to some of the parables that touch our hearts and cause us to think about where we are spiritually. I was not where I needed to be spiritually until one day I read the parable of the good Samaritan again as I had read it many times and all of a sudden I saw me in this parable. I was so much like the priest and the Levite having shirked my responsibility as a Christian.

This parable reminded me of my servant responsibility to others who fall by the wayside or are simply dismissed as not important. Many fall by the wayside because their country has no infrastructure, and oftentimes corruption takes away the food and water, leaving them to crawl around for the crumbs that fall from the tables of politicians. So many who live in third world countries have so little and must scamper around even to find a bite to eat or must drink from some muddy hole if there is even that.

According to the United Nations Food and Agriculture Organization, which measures "under nutrition," there are over 925 million hungry people in the world today. Many will die a terrible death unless someone comes to their aid. According to UNICEF, twenty-two thousand children die each day due to poverty. Often, they die quietly in some of the poorest villages on earth, far removed from the scrutiny and the conscience of the world. Being meek and weak in life makes these dying multitudes even more invisible in death. (UNICEF)

Sad to say, they must suffer and die while the majority of us continue with our self-imposed anxieties. As long as I do not have to look at them or listen to their cries, it is not my problem. The question is, when does it become my problem? Just like the priest and the Levite, when did the man they passed by become their problem? Maybe they thought *As long as I look the other way, he will disappear.*

For one reason or another, many people fall by the wayside receiving very little care or concern from their country. Christian organizations all over the United States spend billions of dollars each year coming to the aid of the poor around the world, and still, it is only a drop in the bucket. Where one is helped, a hundred are standing in line. We cannot help them all, you might say.

So I ask the question, The poor, what are they to do, where are they to go? To answer my own question, that's up to us for we are people of faith. We have been blessed to bless others. We are, according to Jesus, doing only that which is our duty (Luke 6:46). We have all heard it said, "Jesus has no hands but your hands, no feet but your feet, no lips but your lips to do his blessed will." I personally find it very difficult not to try to do something in relieving their pain. Whether I succeed or not, it has always been my conviction that I must do something; I must put forth the effort.

We therefore as Christians have failed in living up to the expectation of God, and this is unacceptable.

This Samaritan man came along and saw the same thing the priest and Levite saw—someone needing a helping hand. Each one of us has witnessed a similar scene, and because of our inaction, the individual was left by the wayside, hoping for a more compassionate person to come along.

As I introduce this book, let's take time to read this soul-stirring parable of our Lord as he attempts to get religious people to live up to their responsibilities and also teach this lawyer a lesson. This parable should stir us up to the point where we cannot sleep nor eat until we have come to grips with our responsibilities if we call ourselves followers of Christ.

> And behold, a certain lawyer stood up and tested Him, saying, "Teacher, what shall I do to inherit eternal life?" He said to him, "What is written in the law? How does it read to you?" And he answered and said, "You will love the Lord your God with all your heart, and with all your soul, and with all your strength, and with all your mind; and your neighbor as yourself." And He said to him, "You have answered right. Do this and you will live." But wanting to justify himself, he said to Jesus, "And who is my neighbor?" And Jesus answered and said, "A certain man went down from Jerusalem to Jericho and fell among thieves, who stripped him of his clothing and wounded him, and departed, leaving him half dead. And by chance there came down that way a certain priest. And when he saw him, he passed by on the other side. And likewise a Levite, when he was at the place came and looked at him, and passed by on the other side. But a certain Samaritan, as he journeyed, came where he was. And when he saw him, he had compassion on him. Then he went to him and bound up his wounds, pouring on oil and wine. And he set him on his own beast and brought him to an inn, and took care of him. Now on the next day he took out two denarii and gave them to the host, and said to him, 'Take care of him. And what more you spend, when I come again, I will repay you.' Now which of these three do you think was neighbor to him who fell among the thieves?" Then he said, "He who showed mercy toward him." Then Jesus said to him, "Go and do likewise."
>
> Luke 10:25–37, KJV

"Go and do likewise!" These words hit me as it did the lawyer, and what amazes me the most, Jesus is coming down hard on religious people—the very individuals who should have stopped and offered help but did not. Perhaps their time was too valuable or they were in such a big hurry getting to an appointment they had no time to take care of the needs of this man, someone who was so insignificant, and because, one reason or another, he did not deserve any of their attention, they just let him lie there and perhaps even die where he lay.

When an opportunity to help someone presented itself, how many times have we reasoned, I will take care of that later? Right now there are other things more pressing we reason.

Perhaps you have been guilty as I have of being a priest or Levite only to pass by on the other side of the road. We do not want to admit it, but we all know it is true. Would we not rather be the Good Samaritan who took the opportunity to do a good deed? Yes, it did cost him a little money and time, but the gratification he felt was worth what he put into it.

Never walk by on the other side of the street when an opportunity to help someone is there. It might not be possible to help, but we have to try. This is one message of this book—try. Do not give the cop-out "I can't." This book is a challenge to all of us people of faith.

So that would bring up a question so many have asked me over the years:

Why did I go into mission work? Humorously, sometimes I ask myself that question. When I am somewhere upriver in the rain forest of Panama, sitting in a dugout, floating down a river with my back and other unmentionables hurting, when I'm blistered and the mosquitoes have been working on me, I ask myself why I put myself through this. I could be back in Alabama, sitting under a shade tree, enjoying some good Alabama sweet tea, and playing with my grandchildren. I could be sitting on the bank of a pond, fishing and relaxing, doing all those things that bring so much enjoyment to our lives. For some reason, I'm floating down this river, eating a can of sausages or sardines with crackers and chasing it with warm water. I am sure I am not the only one who has asked himself or herself that question. However, the reward comes when my boat pulls up to the bank and the children are waiting and someone begins banging on an old piece of metal, letting the village know I have arrived—the gringo with the white hair! They begin hugging me for they are so glad to see me. They are like family I have not seen for a long time. Sometimes they'll bring out a banana or other types of fruit grown locally. It is always a joyous reunion. I stand there for a moment and take it all in and think to myself, *Wow, this is great.* I do not deserve the praise of these people. I am here to help them, but they are helping me for they have made me part of their family and their community. This is the main point I want you the reader to learn from this book, it is not about you, is about the people we came to help and the rewards we get back is far greater than we ever dreamed.

So the question is, why do I do mission work? I had really rather each person who reads this book find the answer, and perhaps you might even discover a reason why you should be doing some of the same things. Perhaps you have never been on a mission trip however after reading of the experiences of others at the end of this book, you might even discover what has been missing for so long. You knew something was missing, you just did not know what it was. Some of the reasons you have never gone on a mission trip might be:

- God, you are asking me to give up my family vacation time.
- To spend my own money going to a place where I do not even know the people nor their culture.

- I cannot speak their language.
- Lord, I don't know where you want me to go.

I'm so much reminded of Moses, who must've had the same attitude when God said to him, "I got a mission, and, Moses, you're just the man for the job. You're the one who is going to lead my people out of Egypt. You are the man who is going to go to Pharaoh and say, 'Let my people go.'" Moses then begins to make the same excuses perhaps you have made why you cannot go. So I am going to let you read the book to discover why I made the decision to be a missionary for I guarantee you will discover some things about yourself. It might even open up a whole new world you did not know existed.

In this book, I will show you how you can find that purpose by serving others. When you read the stories of other people who have had life-changing experiences, perhaps you can find your purpose. Some of those in this book you will read about have had their lives touched or totally changed because someone else cared enough to take the time to make a difference. However, what you are going to discover is that the person doing the giving is blessed far beyond their wildest imaginations.

I am not saying things are going to be easy because as you will discover you will have to get out of your comfort zone even though it is only for a short time. During that short time, a change will come about you that you never expected.

By experience, I can show you how you can be a blessing to others. The stories of some who have received a blessing and for those who have bestowed a blessing will help you start looking for opportunities to serve.

Let us discover together how to change a life.

TO CHANGE A LIFE

"I was hungry and you gave me something to eat, thirsty and you gave me something to drink, naked and you clothed me, sick and in prison and you ministered unto me" (Matthew 25:35 ASV). These are the words of our Lord. "But, Lord, when did we see you in these situations?" And the reply comes back, "As you have done it unto the *least of these*, you have done it unto me" (Matthew 25:40 ASV). We all remember these are the words of Jesus. They are convicting and thought provoking.

My goal in writing this book is to get all of us as servants of God to find a ministry whether it be next door, across town, or in another part of the world. Find a ministry, something beyond yourself. Reach out to the less fortunate and follow the example set before us throughout the Bible as our Lord's ministry developed itself.

Doing things for people without expecting anything in return should be our motto. Dr. Max Edrington, an optometrist from Long Beach, Mississippi, has a saying, "Help others a little and yourself a lot." Life is about helping others, reaching out beyond ourselves. I recently saw a sign with the following words: "You have never really lived until you have done something for someone who cannot repay you." For a person to feel complete, they must learn to give of themselves. This old cliché, "Charity begins at home," is definitely not biblical. Sometimes we become self-centered, thinking that life is all about us. Somewhere, I heard the statement, "Me, my wife, our two children, us four and no more." While someone else said, "Us two and that will do!" If I said that, I would not want anyone to know that was my attitude toward life in general. My late mother, Thelma Brady, wrote the following poem.

Self-Centered

The boy was lost, bewildered and alone:
He needed someone to lean upon.
He was too young to understand
Why you did not offer a helping hand.

The man was old and weak and frail;
He needed warmth against the wintry gale.
You had no time for his aged feet
Shuffling along on the busy street.

Somewhere close you heard the cry
Of a lonely heart as you pass by.
You did not heed the sore distress
Of a voice calling in the wilderness.

You traveled on becoming discontent,
Then found out when your life was spent,
You had failed to leave from day to day
A part of yourself along the way.

You joined the band of the rushing throng
Forgetting all others as you hurried along;
Then you ask yourself the reason why
You have missed so much as life passed by.

We do miss so much of life because so many of us think and reason that we must take care of our own. "Life is all about me and my family and my money is mine for I worked for it. Why should I help others I don't know?" This is the attitude of so many; however, it must not be found among God's children. So many of us think that for us to be truly happy, we must fill our life with things. These people live the life of self-centeredness, forgetting about all others. I cannot say I always had a servant's heart. It calls for me to have a different outlook on all the things I have for now they mean so little and are so insignificant. Having a big bank account is not the most important thing in life. However, learning to share is one of the first attributes Jesus taught each of us by the example he set before us. "Share what we got because we all got a lot," says a song I have heard.

When I first started doing mission work, I really never understood why until one day I saw a man with no legs begging on a street in downtown Panama City, Panama. I had seen him there before with two wooden handles he used to get around. I cannot even imagine what this good man goes through every day of his life just to survive, to have something to eat, and to have a place to sleep. He had a cup in front of him for people to put in some change. I saw what everyone else saw—a person in need. Yet like so many, I looked away so I would not have to look at him nor have to speak to him. There was a Panamanian minister walking with me and saw the same thing I did; however, his response was different than mine. I continued to walk, not noticing he was not with me. When I finally realized I was by myself, I turned around, looking for him. I saw him on his knees in front of the man with no legs. He put some money in his cup, telling him that if he would like to come to church, he would make arrangements to come and get him. I was embarrassed at myself for not being the Christian I should have been. I was no different than anyone else on the street who saw the same thing.

I determined within my heart that day that would never happen again even if it meant me helping someone who did not need it. I had preached the lesson from the parable of the Good Samaritan many times, but evidently, I had not listened to what I preached.

I do not believe Jesus, in teaching us how to be servants, would ever pass up an opportunity to do good. Where you and I cannot perform a miracle, we can use the resources afforded to us in reaching out to others.

People help others in many different ways and come up with their own ideas about how to help.

It is an excuse to say "I cannot help everybody, so I am just not going to help anybody." With this attitude, it would give us a reason not to help those who need it. Others may say, "They're all deadbeats. They ought to get out there and go to work and try to make a living rather than have someone give them everything on a silver platter." I do agree that some people try to get things just because they are free, but at the same time, there are so many people who struggle just to get through the day, and those are the ones Jesus reached out to. In my travels around the world, I have come across many people who did not have the opportunities even to make enough money to buy food for their families. So that's where we come in as Christians—to reach out to help those in need, to change a life. Jesus said, "I have come into the world that you might have life and have it more abundantly" (John 10: 10, KJV). I like that verse because it tells me that Jesus came to teach us about living, what real living is all about. You might say this was the mission statement of Jesus. We are put here to enrich the lives of others. We are to be a blessing to others in some small way. I remember a telephone commercial of years gone by that simply said, "Reach out and touch somebody." It is not as hard as you think to reach out and touch somebody, but it will require some effort on our part. The statement of Jesus of why he came is such a simple statement and to the point. He came to teach us all about life and his purpose.

When Jesus spoke of the abundant life He was not only talking about eternal life but rather is talking about living life to its fullest right now. Jesus calls us to walk as he walked following His example.

He was going about living the abundant life, and much of that was in service to others. It has been wonderful to be part of a mission work that has brought about change to hundreds, if not thousands of lives. All of our efforts are worthwhile when an individual is led into a clinic by his family because he is blind and departs walking, smiling, and rejoicing because a blessing has come into his life. Seeing the reaction of a family as they witness the change because others cared, there are no words to express how it makes you feel. There are so many stories to tell of so many lives changed. It is my prayer that these stories will change your heart, that they will challenge you as an individual to look beyond yourself so you can be a blessing to someone else. Use what God gave you whether small or great. Do not complain about what you do not have, but praise God for what you have and share it. In all of this, you are building relationships that will last a lifetime.

BUILDING RELATIONSHIPS

I have been asked many times, what is the best way to win people to Jesus Christ? I'm sure there has been every gimmick in the world used to get people to believe the way we believe. Many different avenues have been pursued to try to make this happen, to convince people we are the ones they need to follow. Yes, it is important to get people to understand what they need to do to inherit eternal life for this is the ultimate goal of all mission groups.

Although I wonder if we have not gotten the cart before the horse. That is, we go into places and just start preaching away without regard to the fact that many of them are sick and hurting and have so many issues in their lives. Oftentimes they are hungry and thirsty, yet we feel we must get them to obey before we help them. Let me give you an illustration of what I mean for this is a real situation that happened in December of 2010. I arrived in the community of El Salto and found people literally vomiting from having to drink water that even smelled bad for there was none other. I began to visit house to house, listening to the people and seeing the strain on their faces. I thought about Matthew 8 when, after our Lord came down from the mountain, he was immediately approached by a leper who said, "Lord if you are willing make me clean." And the Lord said to him, "I will." Never a word as to what religión this man practiced. When Jesus entered Capernaum a Centurian came to Him saying, "Lord my servant lives at home sick of the palsy and is tormented." Jesus said, "I will come and heal him." He did not discuss the man's religion, only the fact that this man needed help. The people at this community were in desperate need of help. We immediately began making plans to help them in their bad situation. Having said all of this, let me ask you some questions and have you contemplate your answers. How did Jesus begin his ministry? When he went into these communities, what was his first reaction? What was the first thing he did? Jesus was the master teacher, a true missionary with a mission. When each one of us as missionaries lead a team of people into a foreign country, we go there with a mission to teach people about Jesus Christ. The question is, what is the best way for this to happen?

Speaking at a mission seminar, I was asked a question, "Where do you start teaching people?" The first thing I tell people is to follow someone who is already been successful. I believe in following the example of Jesus and reading about the successes he had as he demonstrates to us the proper way. In Matthew 9 and in Matthew 15, the Bible says Jesus came into the communities and towns around, and the multitudes met him as sheep having no shepherd. Jesus was moved with compassion as he looked around at the people.

Think about this question, Do you suppose all the people came to listen to Jesus preach, or had they heard about his ability to restore their health and to supply food for their bellies? We know that the four thousand and the five thousand he fed and the multitudes who came to listen to his message were hungry and needed something to eat. They came to be healed of their illnesses. Many brought their children who had different afflictions and had heard of the Lord and his abilities to take care of all these needs.

Please take a minute as you read this part of this book. Stop for a moment in your reading, close your eyes, and visualize the scene. Jesus has just entered the community, and thousands have gathered. Many had come to see the Master. They had heard of him and desired to see for their own eyes and hear his words and receive a blessing. In your mind's eye, you see the Lord standing there with open arms, looking out over the crowds, and telling the disciples to have the people come closer. "Gather them around for I have compassion on the people for they have been with me three days and have had nothing to eat." All of a sudden, the scene changes, and the disciples say to him, "Lord, we do not have enough food to feed all of these people. Why not just send them away and let them go purchase some food." Jesus replied, "I have compassion on the people. I will not send them away hungry because they will faint in the way. Have them all sit down on the ground. How much food do you have?" The disciples said to the Lord, "Only a few fishes and seven loaves of bread." The Lord offers up a prayer. He breaks the bread and fish, and the disciples begin dividing the food among the crowds. All are fed and are hungry no more. Then the Lord does something else. He begins to take care of their health by healing all manner of sicknesses.

There is another incident in Matthew 20. A scene is unfolding, which I suppose is one of the most moving recorded in the New Testament during our Lord's ministry. The same event recorded here is one that has unfolded literally thousands of times on mission trips around the world. Jesus said to the disciples, "Do not stop the little children from coming unto me for such is the kingdom of heaven." Children were the very center of our Lord's ministry. He used them to demonstrate how his ministry would unfold. Every one of us, as we travel into other countries, are touched by the children, who are so innocent, and usually, they are the ones who are hurt the most in poverty. Each one of us has been touched by children that just sort of hang around where we are working. Therefore, people who travel on mission trips become very attached to the children and desire to do something to make their lives better.

My granddaughter Emma traveled to Panama with her entire family at the age of six and was influenced in a way that will span a lifetime. She met and played all week with Josalina, a child her age who lived nearby. When it came time to depart, they were hugging and crying. They continue a close friendship with Emma. She is saving her change and other items and sends it to her whenever someone goes. This is what true relationships are all about.

So let's answer the question. What is the best way to do evangelism? To lead people to Christ. I believe it is extremely important to build a relationship with the people you're trying to make a difference with. Relationship evangelism begins by letting people see you really care for their situation. It might be they are hungry or sick or perhaps just need somebody to talk to. Let me give you an example:

Diane Edrington a nurse practitioner was preforming pap test in our Sanson clinic for these women have not had the opportunity to be examined for cancer, and this was a godsend for them. She found out as she preformed the examination that most of the women had a story to tell. Diane said many of them just wanted to talk. They had so much on their heart for many were in bad relationships with abusive husbands. Some had different types of infections brought on by these relationships. Up to this time, there had been no one they could talk to, and they needed someone to listen to their problems. Diane said that she just let them talk for it seemed to make them feel better. The kindness, the compassion, and care for someone else's problems oftentimes brings about great results. I believe with all my heart that was one of the secrets to the success of our Lord. Many people just wanted to talk and open their hearts for whatever problem they had. Sometimes we need to listen. Listening and smiling and encouraging can bring such great results when we reach out to the hurting of this world.

Remember, sometimes the greatest evangelism can be listening to someone else and the situations they are facing in their lives, situations that might not seem very important to the listener. Things that seem important to one individual or family may not seem so important to another, but we can listen and let them know we care.

Let me give you some instances of how relationships have changed my life and others servants. Some of these will be humorous and some serious for some of the people I've come in contact with have become very close to me simply because I took the time to listen and to be part of their family. Sometimes I just sit in their home and participate in some activity important to them. One of the great joys I have experienced in this ministry is the times I have been able to visit in the homes of different people, different cultures, and to learn from them. Yes, learn from them for they can teach us so much about their way of life and oftentimes about life itself.

Every tribe of Indians have their own culture, their own language, their own ways of doing things. Within the Darién Province, where most of our ministry is focused, lives the Embera, Kuna, and Wounaan Indians. They love to share their culture and are proud of it. When we go into their villages, we do not seek to change their culture but seek to learn from them as well as them learning from us. I have tried to model this ministry after the ministry of Jesus. Although Jesus knew what the people needed, he always took time with the people, building relationships. Yes, that meant sitting down and eating their food and talking and mingling with them. You will read throughout this book of how people took time to listen and to learn from others, and doing so, we are able to find out what their needs are and how we can help them. In all of this, we are changed because no one can be the same person when you have witnessed another person's poverty and have been part of the correction. You start looking for other ways to help them.

I love this part of my ministry. I even find it fun as I try to become part of the family I am visiting with. I never make fun of their way of life but try to find common ground where we can become friends.

Part of the challenge of this passage lies in the order in which Jesus suggests things be done. This formed part of a common greeting at the time. But it could be much more than a mere verbal punctuation mark. It was a prayer. Does it provoke us about our tendency to pray against things when we begin to think about how to pray for our area, town, or street? Jesus is inviting us to invite him to bring peace to that area. The mere announcement that God's peace is coming to that place is a form of spiritual warfare that drives away destructive forces that may have strongholds there. I find the Indian people become relaxed as we talk about things of interest to them, and when we eat the food they have prepared, it's as though we become part of their culture, even part of their family.

Eating together allowed discussion, perhaps discussing the food we are eating for this signifies acceptance.

This was a redemptive act in its own right when practiced by Jesus with the social outcasts of the day. It reminds us to be with people in the ordinary rhythms of their lives, building friendship and trust. Creating strong friendships depends on mutual care. Jesus asked the Samaritan woman for a drink. He then gave her living water! Jesus prayed for people to be healed. Some were deeply grateful and no doubt became part of his band of followers.

Let me tell you how we won one village over. They did not know what I believed or taught, and I had not discussed it. It was not the proper time nor were they in any frame of mind to listen. It is difficult to sit there and listen to someone discuss religious matters and religious doctrine while holding a child who is vomiting or has a serious case of diarrhea. You're not interested in listening. Their water was bad for they were drinking from the river, and many were sick. I sat there looking at the river, wondering what Jesus would have done in my situation. I was traveling solo on this visit. That is, there were no other North American people with me for my purpose was to help increase their health for the better. I had brought enough water filters to put one in every home. I also had with me twenty-five pounds of rice and four chickens so we could have lunch together. While I prepared the filters, the women began cooking lunch. I had already filtered some water and drank it, demonstrating to them the water was good and refreshing and I was not afraid to drink it. One of the ladies had gone down to the river and brought back a five-gallon bucket of water, and before I could stop her, she started pouring the muddy river water in the clean rice. I said, "Stop, stop, stop please! Let's use clean water." I laughed to myself and thought, *Now this is really dirty rice*. What fun we had, and the rice was good along with the chicken soup the ladies made to go along with it. I knew that as long as the water had boiled, there would be nothing bad in the water, but they did get the sand from the river in it.

When Jesus asked the Samaritan woman for water, he was teaching the disciples a lesson. Jesus didn't send out his followers alone. They ventured into the wider world together. Jesus often met with those considered sinners and publicans in the company of several of his followers. We will not want to face some of the challenges of the culture we live in alone, but we will never change it by hiding in our fancy houses, riding in our fancy cars, and trying to get people to change the way they believe by occasional street preaching or door knocking. If I want people where I preach to pay close attention to me, I say, "Listen to me now." In Spanish, I would say, "Listen to me." So I say to you, the reader, listen to me for the message for each one of us is this: impersonal evangelism may leave the fingerprints of God on someone, but only the friendship that flows from genuine love for others will help this generation feel the embrace of God. People respond to kindness, love, and compassion. For you to be effective, you must demonstrate that which Jesus taught. He taught this to his disciples when they wanted to send everyone away hungry and thirsty.

I have to admit, in the jungles of Panama, I have felt pity upon the people. However, I find that they do not want pity but compassion. Compassion says, "I will help you because you're human, made in the image of God, and worthy of dignity, friendship, and aid." Jesus was color-blind, status-blind, and gender-blind. He didn't see the divisions we often see. He established a church where there is neither Jew nor Greek, male nor female, slave nor free.

Jesus did not come with mere words of wisdom before scurrying home to a spiritual fortress. He lived among and ate with the ordinary people of his day. He was their friend as well as their Savior.

Selfishness indulges self at others' expense. Christianity serves others. Serve! Godliness is shown in godly service to others. People ask me all the time, "How can I help? I live a long way from the people of Panama." Or someone may say, "I live a long way from Africa or Panama and as much as I want to do something I don't believe I could travel and do mission work in a foreign country." My answer to them is, "There is something for everyone in mission work." There are people right next door, across town, in another state that need help. People from all over the country being neighbors and fulfilled what Jesus was talking about. While I am specifically talking about foreign missions and what I have learned and the people I have come in contact with in Panama, I believe people can find a ministry right in their own state, in their own community, at their own backyard.

We found a little neighbor deep in the rain forest of Panama hobbling around on what we thought was a deformed foot and leg. Peter is an odd name for this little guy who does not know what life is like beyond the village of Pina Bijabuao, an Embera community located on the Chucunaque River deep in the rain forest of south western Panama. Our group arrived in the village early in the morning of June 21, 2011, to build on a relationship we had begun back in January when we delivered food. I first met Peter on that trip but did not have the time to talk with him. He was running around with the other kids but could not keep up. I discovered Peter was born with a deformity in his feet. One foot turned in and was smaller than the other one, or at least that is what it looked like. It also seemed that his legs were not the same size; however, when our group returned with a medical doctor in 2012, it was discovered by nurse Jesse Box that there was no deformity in the foot for the problem might even be cerebral palsy. Plans were made to have him transported to the children's hospital in Panama City for further evaluation. But whatever Peter's problem were, it did not slow him down. He was running around laughing and playing, having a good time. This little guy began to touch the hearts of us all. It seems every time I go to a village, something or someone jumps out and grabs me and others with me, causing us to reflect on our own families. Our lives often become so complicated with so many personal issues we fail to realize why we are put here on this earth. Many never get to the point in their Christian walk where they think beyond the borders of their own family. I have no doubt that those who have had the privilege of traveling to some distant primitive culture see life somewhat differently.

When we got out of the boat, we were greeted on the bank by many of the villagers. They looked at us as rich, yet they offered us whatever they had, such as a banana or a pineapple. One Indian lady asked me, "What does it look like on the other side of the river?" I was dumbfounded and could not give her much of an answer for it is difficult to describe something another has never seen. My thoughts were about how much we (North

Americans) take our blessings for granted, such as clean water and plentiful food.

It wasn't until we had left the village that it hit me about how this one little guy affected the group working in the school. How can one so small change so many lives when all he did was run around trying to keep up with the other kids.

Perhaps each one of us should find a Peter to help us reflect on our own lives. The name is not as important as the impact each of us can have on the lives of others. I am afraid we get so tied up in our own self-inflicted problems we forget other people who struggle just to get through the day. We even get angry over small things that have no significance. When this happens we allow the devil to destroy all the good that was done. Do not allow the devil to take away your good-neighbor status.

I may never go on a mission trip. I may never have traveled outside the United States to share my faith, but who I am truly makes a difference in the lives of others. I do not believe this book would be complete if after reading everything in it, you have not come to grips with who you are as a Christian. Each one of us has faced certain events, certain things in our lives that have influenced us as we influence other people. As we share our faith, as we give a cup of cold water in the name of Christ, let others know who we are and what we are all about. Let us not have the wrong motive for what we are doing. Our religion, our faith, do you feel in your own heart it is worth sharing? For if you are not convicted, then how can you convict someone else? It will be shown everywhere you go and in all of your actions.

Someone sent me a funny story of a lady in a beautiful car driving down the street. Someone accidently pulls out in front of this lady, so she pulls up beside them at the next traffic light and began screaming at them and cursing, holding up her fist and making vulgar gestures. She is so angry she keeps it up at the next traffic light when a policeman pulls up behind her. The light turns green, and she takes off very fast, undoubtedly still angry. The policeman turned on his blue lights and pulled her over. There are two policemen; one walks up to the passenger side and one toward the driver side. The lady is ordered out of the car, where she is handcuffed and placed in a police cruiser. She angrily asked the policeman, "Why are you doing this?" Of which he replied, "We have been following you for quite some time and noticed you had a bumper sticker that said 'Follow me to church.' We thought, surely no Christian reacts this way, and you have a bumper sticker indicating you are a member of a local church, so we thought the car was stolen." Have you ever reacted this way?

I was in Walmart and, having purchased only a few items, I went to the express line. All of us have seen the express line sign that says "Twenty items or less." Now there is an individual in the line who has sixty items or more, and those waiting in line behind this individual are becoming angry. When their time comes, they began having a confrontation with the individual at the cash register about why she allowed this person in the first place. Another day gone bad!

We all have, at some point in time, seen this repeated over and over, and it makes you wonder who these people are. Are they Christian? Do they attend church every Sunday? In a recent sermon, I made the point that as a Christian, we should be the same people whether we are on a mission trip or at the movie theater or just having dinner with friends. Perhaps we are sitting in the house of some Indian family on a river in the rain forest. It does not matter where you are; we should let people see Jesus in us.

IT IS MORE BLESSED TO GIVE THAN TO RECEIVE

A young lady in her twenties comes into our clinic to visit our dentist, Dr. Tim Holloway with three of her front teeth broken off. All she wanted was to get them pulled, but this was not what this servant dentist had in mind. He told her, "Let's think about this for a moment." He checked to make sure the teeth were okay and the roots were strong. Finding this all good, he went to work. When he was completed with a buildup on these three front teeth, she was beautiful and could not believe the blessing that had come into her life. She was emotional by what had been done for her. Someone she had not met before and did not know her was this dentist from Pennsylvania using his God-given skills to bring about the greatest change in this young woman's life, and what a change it was. Not only did he bring a change to her life but he and his wife Sharon were changed as this beautiful lady departed the clinic with an extraordinary smile upon her face.

In a world where it seems everyone is out to get all they can without regard for others, it is a good feeling to see people give of themselves in behalf of others. Many people have asked me to put in words the stories of people who have had their lives changed in both the United States and in Panama. However, there are people serving others all over the world, bringing about change, so others can have a better day. Operation Smile and Doctors without Borders are some that come to my mind. Whether a doctor is using his or her God-given skills to help someone feel better or giving people clean water thus changing their lives forever, who receives the greater amount of change, the one who is giving or the one who receives?

As you read the stories of ordinary people being servants, follow their example and join their ranks and become a servant. Whether young or old, you can become a servant. You can make a difference whether small or great for we all can be part of the process of helping someone have a better day.

I heard a fable about a small tack being a part of a beautiful church building. One day, this tack became troubled and began to talk to himself. He said, "I'm just a small tack holding on this shingle every day. My job is not that important." He is so upset because of the small job he is doing he pulls himself out and falls to the ground below. As time went on, the shingle became loose, and rain leaked in and destroyed the beautiful interior of the building—all because a little tack felt useless.

As a minister, I have listened to members make similar statements. "I feel as though I am not needed here," some say. Sometimes we think God is going to look more favorable on the big things people do, and the small things fall by the wayside. The church is made of diverse people, people with many types of gifts! The point is, all can do something, be it small or large. God gave each one of us talents—some few and some many for we are all different. In Romans 12, Paul talks about the transformed life and what it means, and then, in verse 3, he talks about for us not to think more highly of ourselves than we ought to think but think soberly and Godly. In the next few verses, he says that everybody has a diversity of gifts. Some can teach, some can make dresses, and some might even be a president or hold some other high office. Never think you are better than anyone else for you just have a God-given gift that God expects you to use.

Paul continues to talk about people finding their ministry. The sad commentary is so many never find their ministry and are always searching. You and a doctor may not have the same ministry but both are important. It might be holding a baby that comes into the clinic for a mother who is being attended to.

On a recent trip, two high school students, Catherine Sales from Jonesboro, Arkansas, and Ragan Stone from Walnut Ridge, Arkansas, were working with the doctors when a baby was brought in with 105 degree temperature and was not breathing very well. Something had to be done and fast. What could they do in all of this? A large pan was brought in, and Catherine and Ragan submerged the child, putting cool water over the baby, thus being part of saving this baby's life. They learned that day what it meant to be a servant.

As we give of ourselves in behalf of others, our lives will change, and then we will always look for other opportunities to do good—just like Jesus. For Jesus said in Acts 10:35, "It is more blessed to give than to receive."

Growing up on a farm in the Pintlala community in central Alabama, there were many things I learned, but little did I know as to how those things I learned on the farm could be applied to my Christian life many years later. My father was a simple man who never owned a car, a telephone, or a television. He wore overalls all his life. On Sunday, he would put on a Sunday suit, Sunday shoes, take his hat out of the box he had it stored in, and off he would go to church. Seeing my father always giving food away would have a great impact upon me. We did not have inside bathroom facilities or running water nor any of the things so many hold so dear however we had the necessities of life.

This reminds me of the Macedonians in 2 Corinthians 8, when the Bible says, "Though they were in *deep poverty* they gave beyond their ability to give." Being poor is not a reason not to help others. Jesus said of the woman with the alabaster box who had come to anoint him, "She has done what she could." God only expects us to do what we can. My dad, through example, taught us to do what we could with what we have. One man said at Dad's funeral, "He gave tons of food away even under hard times." Yes, each one of us must learn this fine art of giving, of serving, following the example of Jesus, our Master. I'm sure each one would have his or her story as to how they became a servant. However or wherever you learned it, it all goes back over two thousand years ago when God gave his only begotten son (John 3:16).

TO FULFILL A COMMAND

Before we can learn what it is that drives people in the giving of themselves, going out of their way to help those we do not know, we need to first look at the person of Jesus. People respond better with kindness, to a sweet disposition than to a mean-spirited person. This is why people wanted to be close to Jesus for he was enjoyable to be around.

There is something here I have overlooked for so long in my ministry. We are commanded to fulfill certain commands throughout the Bible. We can not pick and choose the ones that suit us. One command all religious people know by heart is "Go into all the world and preach the gospel" (Matthew 28:19–20, Mark 16:16, ASV).

Let's look at this command and answer the question as to the best reason one should fulfill it. If you have been on a mission trip, why did you go? Think about it! Why did you choose to go with your church or someone else on a mission trip? Was it based upon being commanded to go or some other motivation?

Let's look at two people who, for very different reasons, traveled on a mission trip.

The first one arrives at the destination and immediately begins to complain. "It's hot. I don't understand anything they are saying. They drive me crazy with all their jabbering. There is no order in their driving. In the United States, at least they would get a ticket. I hate the culture. All these people want is a handout."

And on and on it goes. Someone says, "Why in the world did you come? The reply may shock you. The individual says, "The Bible commands us to go into the entire world to preach, and I am here to fulfill that command. I do not have to like it, but I am going to do my duty because God said to do it." Shocked! Oh yes, I had an individual who traveled with me many years ago with that attitude. Did the people pick up on it? Yes, they wanted to know what was wrong with him.

Another Christian arrives and is always smiling, even trying to converse and had fun doing it. The attitude is one with Jesus's as he went about seeking to fulfill the will of the Father. Remember what Jesus said, "My will is to do the will of my Father." This second individual has arrived for the same purpose as the first one, just with a different attitude. He desires to carry out the commands of Jesus with an attitude of love and compassion, following the example of Jesus.

In my opinion, the worst reason I know for doing mission work is the command to do it. We *must* fulfill God's will but by following the example of our Lord. Jesus desires that we love him with all out heart, soul, mind, and strength and to love our neighbors as ourselves (Matthew 22:37-40).

To the average onlooker, it does not seem logical one would intentionally leave the comforts of home and travel to some third world country when there is a lot to do next door. The question is easily answered when the individual asking the question is finally convinced to go on a mission trip, and now they cannot wait until next year when they can return.

Whatever the motivation that causes one to help the unfortunate, whether doctor, nurse, dentist, or helper, it brings about a change that is hard to put in words. It is my desire to write about the people that I went to help who did more for me than I ever did for them. They always thank us for coming, but it is those of us who go who should be saying thank you.

This book is about the results of simply following the example of Jesus. Growing up in the small community of Pintlala, Alabama, a small community fifteen miles south of Montgomery on US Highway 31, I never dreamed of where the future would take me. Over the course of my life, I have been privileged to travel a lot. It has been a wonderful journey with many experiences along the way. Being the middle son of eleven children, I do not believe I was prepared for what the future had in store for me. I learned as I traveled throughout the world about different cultures and how they were so much different than life in a small community. One thing I did learn and quickly, we all have the same needs and desires. The more I studied of Jesus and His ministry the more I wanted to be like Him. You might say I learned from Jesus how to serve. However, what I want to write about is not so much about what Christian life is all about but what it has to offer when we look beyond ourselves. The Christian life is far more than going to church every Sunday and fulfilling the responsibility that we feel. I believe it is far more than getting up on Sunday morning and going down to the meeting house and going through the acts of worship. Yes, this is very important! We go to church because we want to praise and pay adoration to our God. It is the highlight of my week to have the opportunity to get up on Sunday morning or Sunday night or Wednesday night whenever the opportunity affords itself and worship my God.

I became a Christian at age sixteen and have been in and out of church until one day it dawned on me that I was wasting so much of my life. It was time to move on and do something better. I did not dream as to where it would take me. I simply had a desire to preach and found it was something I love doing. I have always enjoyed meeting people, which is so much what mission work is all about. I did not know what or how God could use me in his kingdom. I only knew that I wanted to do something and there had to be some life changing before I could make a difference in anyone else's life.

In a conversation with a young missionary in Panama, he made a statement that was powerful. He said an individual had a talk with him about his desire for Jesus to be his Savior. He asked this person, "Is Jesus the Lord of your life?" His replied, "I just want him to be my Savior." The young missionary said, "He cannot be your Savior if he is not the Lord of your life."

Before one can help others change their lives for the better, they first must make changes in their own lives, changes like putting God first, reaching out to others before thinking of yourself. These are all things I've wrestled with all my life. Sometimes we reach out and we do things for the wrong reason, the wrong motive, and everything falls by the wayside.

For a long time, I preached in small congregations, doing what I thought was what God wanted me to do. I found it very easy to meet people regardless of their circumstances and regardless of their standing in the community. Rich or poor, black or white, I did not have problems meeting people. As a matter of fact, I love meeting people and have always felt that that was my calling. I had to be taught what God wanted me to do. I had to learn, and sometimes, it was the hard way. The disciples of our Lord were chosen because they had what Jesus was looking for. The question is, what does he look for? What did he look for in the disciples when he first chose Peter, Andrew, James, John, and all the others? What did he see in these men as he walked by them as they were mending their nets. They were fishermen, tax collectors, positions from all walks of life. Isn't it amazing he did not choose them because of their financial standing in the community nor for their political view but, rather, he chose them because of what he saw in them? What did God see in me? What does God see in you that would cause him to have you or me go to the mission field?

I am always amazed every time I read the story of Jesus feeding the five thousand with such a small amount of food. Why? Because the disciples were so much like you and me? Listen to them! "Lord, there are a lot of people here. Where are we going to get enough food for so many people? Send them away so they can find them something to eat and drink." Those are the words of the disciples who were so close to him. They are learning now from the Master just as you and I learn from him.

In Matthew 15:32, Jesus said, "These people have been with me for three days and I have compassion upon them because for they are hungry and *I will not* send them away fasting because they will faint in the way." Powerful words, are they not? Convicting words for people who should have known what to do yet we all have to learn what God expects of each one of us. That's a good question, isn't it? What does God expect out of Larry Brady? What does he expect out of any of us? No, he does not expect every person to go into the mission field in some faraway land and live in difficult circumstances, giving up all the comforts of life. But he does expect each one of us to have a giving heart, to have a compassionate, loving, kind, and generous heart. He does expect each one of us to find our ministry.

> Having then gifts differing according to the grace that is given to us, whether prophecy, *let us prophesy* according to the proportion of faith; or ministry, *let us use it* in *our* ministering; or he who teaches, in teaching; or he who exhorts, in exhortation; he who gives, *let him do it* with liberality; he who leads, with diligence; he who shows mercy, with cheerfulness.
>
> Romans 12: 7, ASV

Each one of us has something we can do in the kingdom of our Lord. If you have not found yours, please find it. It might not be in a public way. Your ministry might be helping someone else be a missionary or collecting medicine for the medical team.

We are expected to set our priorities correctly and not live like the rich young ruler who came running to Jesus, desiring to know what he had to do to go to heaven. He had everything money could buy, but he did not have the very thing that Jesus wanted him to have—a giving and sacrificial heart. Jesus knew his heart and tells him to go sell all that he has given to the poor and take up his cross and follow him. Jesus did not want all that he had; he just knew that it was the money, the things in his life that was keeping this young man from heaven, from reaching that ultimate goal that we all so much desire.

In this book, perhaps you will find your calling. Perhaps you will find your ministry for all of us who have made Jesus the Lord of our lives desire so much to have a ministry. What is your ministry?

YOU BUY MY SISTER

When I was a child growing up in the Pintlala community, little did I realize what road or roads I would travel down over the course of my life. We all have dreams and aspirations as to what we would like to be or what we would like our children to be. We read of people who have had great adventures, and we think if we could do something like that someday, but never in our wildest imagination do we ever believe that will ever happen. Sometimes it's because of the surroundings in which we grew up. I do not know how many times I have heard people say "I would've never thought Larry Brady would've ever become a missionary." To be honest with you, I would not have thought it either.

I was the middle child of eleven children. My father farmed and worked as a house painter while my mother worked as a waitress in Montgomery. My older sisters would be the ones to take care of us smaller children while Mom and Dad worked to make a living. It was a good life, and we were happy until one day, our house caught on fire. I was six years old at the time. My father sat outside all night, watching the house smolder, not knowing where we would all live. It was a great burden to not know how he was going to take care of his family. However, all of us went to live with different people throughout the community until Dad was able to build our new house across the road from our old house. In several months, this house was finally completed, and we all moved in. It did not have heat or air-conditioning or indoor facilities. We did have electricity but no television or telephone. We had what we needed.

Looking back over my life, I wonder if God was preparing my heart to become a missionary heart. No, I do not believe everyone needs to be born poor in order to be a servant, but I do believe all need to learn what Jesus was trying to teach.

Jesus was the perfect example for you and me because he understood our situations.

When I turned eighteen, I decided to join the United States Air Force during the height of the Vietnam War in 1966. In late 1968, I got my orders to report to Travis Air Force Base outside of San Francisco, California. I was a country boy with a tenth grade education and had never traveled outside the state of Alabama. I grew up on a small farm south of Montgomery, Alabama. My dad continued asking me, "Son, are you sure this is what you want to do?" My friends were all joining the military, and I thought this is something I wanted to do. I always saw those big airplanes fly over and thought, *I sure would like to work on one of those.* I had no mechanical knowledge of even a bicycle, but I thought it sure would be neat just to work on one of those airplanes. I had read that if you really wanted to work on airplanes, you needed to join the air force, so that's what I did. I reported to Travis Air Force Base in November of 1968. I got on that big jet airplane for the fifteen-hour flight to Bangkok, Thailand. To be honest with you, I had never even heard of Bangkok, Thailand. I knew little of the Vietnam War, only what I've heard the short time I had been in the military, and I knew the possibility I would wind up in Vietnam was very good. However, my assignment took me to a place called Nakhon Phanom, Thailand. This was located only eight miles from the Mekong River, which bordered Laos.

Arriving in Bangkok, it usually took about three days to process everyone for their trip up country to their base, which would be home for the next twelve months. During these three days, we were all put in a hotel in downtown Bangkok and were allowed to see the sights. For someone coming out of the community of a couple hundred people into this huge city of millions, it is quite scary, to say the least. I began walking around, looking at the sights. It was unlike anything I had ever seen. Also, it would be here in this big city I would have my first contact with real poverty. I always thought we were poor until this day. It was amazing to see all the boats floating about and everyone doing their trading. It was called the floating market where everyone brought their fruits and vegetables and meats and other things to sell. Standing there, looking with amazement, two children approached me. I just stood there not knowing what to say because I had only been there one day and knew nothing of the language. I learned, as all do, a few words as time went on. They came up to me, putting their hands together in front of them as though they were praying, and bowed before me, which meant good morning.

I just stood there dumbfounded. I do not even know if I responded because I did not know what they were saying to me and had never had anyone bow to me. I really thought that maybe this was some type of religious thing. I was that dumb. Later, after we arrived at our base, we were briefed on culture. If I had read the material the military had given me that was back in my hotel room, I would know that this was a greeting for morning, noon, and night. One thing I did learn, everyone everywhere understands a little bit of English, and it was no exception with these two children. Something else I came to understand—Americans are considered rich people around the world, especially in poor countries. People have the idea that money grow on trees and all you have to do is go out and pick some of it. We do not realize how blessed we are to live in the United States of America. Even with the problems we have, it is nothing like what people in other countries live in every day.

What happened next shook me. I did not know what to do nor what to say, so I didn't say anything nor did I do anything. I just stood there in front of two children who were perhaps the dirtiest children I had ever seen in my life. They had no shoes and were dressed very poorly. Oriental people are beautiful people, and I do remember this little girl standing next to her brother was beautiful with her coal-black hair although a mass of tangles. This image burned in my mind and has never left it. Perhaps this is what motivated me in years to come because I would always remember these two children standing there looking at me, a nineteen-year-old from South Alabama, as though I could be there savior on this day. What this little boy said next shook me up to the point that many years later, when I stood in the streets of Panama City, Panama, I thought of these two children. I made up my mind on that day in 1984 in Panama City, Panama, that I would return to Panama and try my best to make a difference in the lives of as many people as I could. Little did I realize where that decision would take me and how many others would be affected by my personal decision. I do not believe anyone realizes how their personal decisions will affect others. Our everyday decisions affect someone somewhere.

The little boy said over and over, I remember the words, even the words in Thai, "My sister, you want?" His sister was about ten years old, I estimated, and was very small. He pointed at his stomach indicating he was hungry. And then, in almost perfect English, he said, "You buy my sister for 100 baht." Five dollars for his sister! He was willing to sell his sister to me for five dollars. I didn't say anything because I didn't know what to say. After I left and was back at my hotel room, I begin to think, *Why did I not just give them five dollars?* I had the money in my pocket even though in those years we did not make a lot of money, but I could have afforded five dollars. This would make a tremendous impact upon me in years to come.

How would Jesus have reacted in my situation? There is no doubt in my mind what he would've done. He would have taken care of this child. He would have given them food, and then he would have taken them somewhere where they could receive proper care. He would not have allowed them to stand there hungry. Perhaps this is what has caused me to become a missionary.

I chose the Republic of Panama. Someone else chose Guyana, Columbia, or some other third world country where people are hurting. Others have chosen the ghettos in the United States of America. There are a lot of hurting people who need our help every day across the street or down the road. Yes, perhaps some of it is of their own making; however, this does not release each one of us from our responsibility to make a difference in the lives of others. I determined never to go by on the other side of the road when it's within my ability to make a difference in someone's life.

Returning home to Pintlala, Alabama, after my time in the Vietnam War was over, I could not get the image out of my mind of that little girl so many years ago with those beautiful eyes standing there in the streets of Bangkok. I've often wondered what she and her brother turned out to be, what happened to them. I even thought that if I had just taken an interest in that little girl, perhaps her life would be different today. Does she remember me standing there with a shocked look on my face and wonder why this American did not at least give them a little food? You see, the air force had given me enough money for my travel expenses. I had enough money in my pocket to have relieved their hunger pains, and I did nothing.

A BOY WHO LOST A DOLLAR

I am sure I am like so many others when faced with certain events in their lives—we soon forget. We forget how God delivered us and brought us home safely. Maybe we even forget our prayers we so often pray when we ask God for so many things and make promises to him, and when he fulfills his promises, we forget ours. We forget his goodness, his compassion, and his mercy toward us when it comes our turn.

Go back and read the story from the book of Exodus, and perhaps you will see some of us in those people. God gave them all they needed to make the journey from Egypt to the promised land, and no sooner than they departed that they began to cry out how they would be better off in Egypt than living on the bread and water God had given them to sustain them while on their journey. God chose Moses to lead his people out of bondage in Egypt, where they had been for 430 years (Exodus 12:41). In their travels, not only did the Lord provide food for their bellies but protection from the army of Pharaoh. When the people cried out in fear, the Lord heard their cry. When they cried out from hunger, the Lord heard their cry. Yes, they were crying out to the Lord for help, and he helped them, not once but many times—even when they didn't deserve it.

We read of God's mercy in Luke 17:12 in the story of ten men who were lepers. They cried out to the Lord, "Jesus Master have mercy on us." They are healed of this terrible disease, and as they walk, they see they are clean. One who was looking down, seeing he is healed, went back and gave glory to God, and the words of Jesus were, "Were not ten cleansed, but where are the nine?"

I returned home from Thailand and went back to my old way of living even though the image of the little girl and her brother never left my mind for very long. It was placed in the back of my mind, and often I would remember the two children with such sad eyes. I went on with my life until eleven years later, standing in the streets of Panama City, Panama, I reflected back over my life and made a determination to give my life in service to others. With five children at home, my wife and I made the determination to be servants, true servants. Why did it take so long? All those years I could have served. I cannot change the past but can make the future.

None of us can go back into the past, but we should strive to make a difference in the lives of someone somewhere. I tell people, "You are helping people you will never meet this side of eternity." There are so many people that need help, and what if it is only you who could give them that help? This is a very solemn question each one of us should ask ourselves.

Each Christian must find their ministry. What will that ministry be? Perhaps it's helping serve the poor in the soup lines of local ministries in your town or becoming involved in your church in helping those in your community. Perhaps it might even be of service to the homeless, the orphaned children. Whatever it is, everyone should find a ministry.

I read a story one time of a man whose life was miserable. I do not even remember where I read it, and I have used it in my preaching because it reminds me of how small things can make a difference. This man had everything going for him. He had wealth, a good family, a good community, food on the table every night. Everything we hold so dear, this man had, except he had never learned to serve.

It came time for him to go home from work, and as he was departing his building, he saw a little boy crying while standing on the curb. He felt he could not just go away without at least trying to find out what was going on. He goes up to the little boy and says to him, "Son, what's wrong?" The little boy looks up through his tears and said, "My daddy sent me to the store to get a loaf of bread with a dollar, and I lost the dollar." The man reached into his pocket and pulled out a dollar and gave it to the little boy. The little boy grabs this man around the legs, saying, "Mister, I wish you were my daddy." Someone later asked him, "What did you do?" He simply said, "I drove around, looking for another little boy who lost a dollar."

Perhaps all of us should go around looking for a little boy who lost a dollar. How each person determines to be a servant must be within their own mind because everyone's ministry is different. Let me relate to you, the reader, some examples of people who have related to me why they pursued their area of ministry.

A knock came on my door, and when I opened it, I saw two small children standing there. They asked, "Do you have any old papers, lady?" I wanted to say no, but I invited them in and made them some hot chocolate and toast to warm them up.

The little boy standing there next to the fire asked, "Lady, are you rich?"

"Rich," she replied, "my, no, I'm not rich. Why do you ask?"

"Your cups match your saucers."

"My cups match my saucers!" I had never thought about that, And then they left, holding their papers against the wind.

She said, "Their footprints were still wet about my hearth, so I left them there to remind me of how rich I am. My husband with a good steady job, potatoes and brown gravy, a roof over my head, these things matched too."

Through these two children she found her ministry in her senior years and started helping people who were cold and needed something to eat, and a hot drink.

Perhaps she is remembering the words of Jesus recorded in Matthew 25 when he said, "I was hungry and you fed me. Thirsty and you gave me something to drink. Naked and cold and you clothed me. Sick and in prison and you visited me." This lady might say to the Lord, "Lord, when did I see you in just such a situation." His reply would be, "As you have done it to the *least of these*, you have done it to me" (Mathew 25:40, KJV). This statement of Jesus is very powerful. A statement that convicts our hearts, a statement that I have read over and over and have included in this book several times. It moves us to action causing each one of us to say, "How can I sit on the sidelines and look on when there are so many lives to touch?"

FINDING A MINISTRY

As my travels took me to many locations throughout the world, it wasn't until 1984 when I found the place where my ministry would begin. It was not what I expected. As a matter of fact, I don't know what I expected. I remember getting off the C-130 military transport airplane at Howard Air Force Base, Panama, on a very hot and muggy day on July 12. Standing there on the tarmac, I looked around at the tropical setting, not realizing this was going to be the beginning of a ministry that would span nearly three decades. During those three decades, thousands of lives would be changed, but more especially, the one who received the greatest change was Larry Brady. And what a change it would be for it was not in the way I expected. None of us know how God is going to use us in his kingdom; we just need to be ready for whatever he sends our way. I do not know if I was ready but soon found where I really wanted to be and what I wanted to do. So often, people tell me they cannot go or they do not have the money to go, and all the excuses begin to roll out. I tell them that the hardest thing about going on a mission trip is making the decision to go for when that decision is made, the money is not difficult to get.

I arrived in the midst of the rainy season. There were funny little animals I saw outside the barracks; I did not know what they were. I do not even know their correct names but they had these long tails, so at first I thought they were monkeys, but I learned very quickly they were not monkeys but something everyone called Cucamonga. They were everywhere and did not seem to be overly concerned with people. There were many birds, from parakeets to those that I do not have a name for. This also was in the midst of mango season. I would later fall in love with the flavor of this very sweet fruit from this tropical paradise. I saw my first coconut tree and was told never to stand under a coconut tree for very long for obvious reasons. At the encouraging of some of my fellow workers from the base, I tried to climb a coconut tree; however, I found out it was not so easily done. Yes, there was so much I wanted to see, and I wasted no time.

I found the church where I attended worship, which happened to be in the very center of what was called the Panama Canal Zone.

> The Panama Canal Zone was a 553-square-mile unorganized U.S. territory located within the Republic of Panama, consisting of the Panama Canal and an area generally extending five miles on each side of the centerline, but excluding Panama City and Colón, which otherwise would have been partly within the limits of the Canal Zone. Its border spanned two of Panama's provinces and was created on November 18, 1903 with the signing of the Hay-Bunau Varilla Treaty. When reservoirs were created to assure a steady supply of water for the locks, those lakes were included within the Zone. http://en.wikipedia.org/wiki/Panama_Canal_Zone

What a magnificent undertaking when I finally had an opportunity to visit the Panama Canal. It was more than I had ever thought or dreamed it would be, and to be able to stand there and look out over this wonder of the world was truly a great opportunity. As great as that was, it was not the experience that would cause me to return to Panama time and time again over the next twenty-nine years.

On Sunday morning, someone came by the barracks and picked me up for worship service. I loved the experience of being there and told everyone I thought it must've been something like a turn-of-the-century church we read about in Acts 2. The Bible says there were many different languages there. In this church, there were people from literally all over the United States and from Panama. There were black and white, Indian and Panamanian, all worshiping together.

After worship service, a little lady came up to me and introduced herself. "I'm Sister Amy," she said. I looked at her and immediately fell in love with this sweet little lady who was so poor. I learned as time went on about the heart of Sister Amy. I returned the next year to speak in a revival service for this church, and Sister Amy and I bonded. Every time she came into service, she always had some cookies she had baked for me. She also had some fruit in a bag to give to someone else. Sister Amy lived quite a ways from the church building and would have to catch one of the local buses called Chiva bus, which would drop her off on the main highway. She walked up the hill and down the next to the church building, carrying a bag. No one really knew how old Sister Amy was. Some thought she might be close to one hundred. She did not even know how old she was. She would come up to me and say, "God bless you, Brother Brady." She was very small, perhaps five feet tall, and slender and wore a red wig. It was actually more orange, I suppose, than red, but in any case, she looked her best. She loved me, and I love her. She always was happy to see me return to Panama and never forgot me. She was the first Panamanian I had anything to do with, and she taught me so much. Looking at Sister Amy, I thought to myself, what can I do to help change the lives of people like her who live in such deep poverty? The answer was not what I expected. It was me who received so much. I am the one who was helped by this small lady who had so little from a material standpoint but had so much more from her Christ like life. If we will just take the time, we can learn so much from others who we sometimes think are so insignificant. They touch our lives in ways we never expect. We become better people, better servants as we watch and learn. Never become so arrogant to think you cannot learn. We learn by observing the actions of others. I am afraid we as North Americans think we are the ones who will teach others to be like us, but we do not realize that the simple ways of others are oftentimes much more powerful. Yes, Sister Amy taught me so much, and it changed the course of my ministry.

I suppose one of the first things I learned was that we North Americans do not always have the best answers. We can learn from others.

Let me explain why I refer to those who live in the United States as North Americans. I made the same mistake so many have made in referring to the people who live in Central and South America. I would say, "We Americans." I was corrected by a young person who said, "I am an American." I had not even let that cross my mind. She was right. She was from Central America, so now I make sure I refer to those of us from the United States as North Americans. Perhaps this is another lesson that we all should learn as we travel throughout the world, that God does not prefer those who live in the United States. Just because we live in United States does not make us closer to God and have easier access. So often, those who live in other parts of the world and in deep poverty are better stewards than we are. Materially, they have so little; spiritually, they are so strong. Yes, we can learn much from others around the world that have so little in their lives.

A GREAT AND EFFECTUAL DOOR

I arrived in Panama City on a mission trip to work with a church located in the Canal Zone. However, on this trip, I was met at the airport by some ministers who were working with different churches in the city. They had an offer for me I was somewhat nervous about. They asked me about traveling with them to the Darién Province. The Darien province, I did not like the sound of that for I had heard so many bad thing about this part of Panama. This is the last province in Panama traveling southeast toward Columbia. None of what I had heard was good. Everything was dangerous. The rebels from Columbia roving about might kidnap you and take you into Columbia. The Indians did not always like people coming into their villages. I did not know whether I wanted to go but decided to drive down the road and see what happens.

We needed a four wheel drive vehicle due to bad roads. I found out this was an understatement as I began driving down the Pan-American Highway. I could not find a 4×4 to rent for they needed to be reserved. I had to settle for a small car. We looked like sardines; however, the four of us piled into this car and headed out for a great adventure.

All over Panama, the police have checkpoints. I have never understood why there are so many checkpoints, but they have them. They like to see your passport or your driver's license or just whatever would strike their fancy at that time. Sitting there at the checkpoints in Chepo, the policeman asked, "where are you going?" I said, "To the town of Torti." To which he replied, "In this car." When he said this, I should have known there must be a problem. He indicated for me to pass on through, which I did. We got about four miles down the road when the pavement ran out, and about another mile, we came to a metal bridge with part of it missing in the middle and a big drop-off of about fifty feet below us. I got across the bridge and stopped, and I inquired of my host, "Are we going to be able to make it?" The reply to me was, "No problem. We travel this way all the time." The road continued to get increasingly worse with big rocks hitting the bottom of the small car. I could only imagine what it was doing to the oil pan and to the gas tank. I was driving along at about two miles an hour, just barely creeping to try not to destroy this little rental car.

About three hours later, we had come about twenty-five miles to an Indian community at a big metal bridge that spanned Lake Bayano. This lake would be our focal point in the future for when we reached the big metal bridge, we were almost at the end of the dirt road. There was a large Kuna Indian community here, so we just decided we would stop and visit with them for a while. There also was another police checkpoint where all of our documents were checked and inquiries were made as to where we were going and how long we would be there. The police again had a good laugh, I am sure, at my ignorance, but this time, I made some more inquiries. After a break, I inquired of my host how much further it was to Torti. I was told it was about forty miles. To which I replied, "I think we need to return to the city and regroup because I really do want to return this car to the rental company in one piece." We did return to Panama City and regroup and continued with the mission that I had come to Panama for in the first place. However, the following year, I made plans and reserved a really nice 4×4 that would make the trip into the deep interior, thus leading me down a wonderful road of friendships and some of the most life-changing experiences I would ever make. It would lead me to many different people that affected hundreds of lives throughout the United States.

God often leads us on journeys that we do not understand why and for what purpose they might be. The journeys are not always easy. Sometimes these journeys lead down long hot, dusty roads and across mountains and through valleys. If we really have a desire to learn about mission work, how to change lives, and how to deal with people, follow the Apostle Paul as he made his journeys. Paul was not experienced and had not been to any school to teach him how to do mission work, but rather, God led him, and he learned all along the way. When he began his three missionary journeys recorded in the book of Acts, he never realized what road or roads he would travel and the people he would meet along the way. Paul only knew that God had a mission for him, and he went forth to fulfill that mission. You can begin reading in Acts 13 about the missionary journeys of this great missionary and how he taught us so much. Look at the variety of people he came in contact with along the way. He, like so many of us, stayed in homes, enjoying the hospitality of many different categories of people. He definitely was a people person, and he loved them, and they loved him. He would later write in a number of his epistles how he longed to be with his brethren. He thanked God for just the remembrance of them and always waited and longed for the next time he would be there with them.

On one of these journeys, Paul said, "A great and effectual door has been opened unto me"(1 Corinthians 16:9, KJV). The Apostle Paul had an opportunity to minister to the people at Ephesus, a very populous city where he hoped great good would be done. While at Ephesus, Paul used the opportunity God had given him to preach the Gospel to those who were there, and many came, and their hearts were opened to it. The Bible says a great number believed and obeyed. Yes, the Apostle Paul went through the door God opened for him, giving him reasons to tarry there.

As for me, I felt something similar to what Paul did because as I have journeyed throughout this beautiful country and not only Panama but throughout the world, I have found wonderful people who are in search for what lies ahead for them. The apostle Paul on his journeys must have felt like I did as I arrived in Torti. Sitting there in my vehicle in the middle of a dusty road, I thought, God has opened a door for this great ministry.

I, like the apostle, was making use of what was before me. Satan always places obstacles in our way as we preach the gospel and with great success for many quit before they even get started.

Within me, I tried to come up with many reasons why I should not return to Panama but I could find no good reason and could not allow the devil to control the things that I would do nor the impact that I would have upon the people there. When God opens a door, he expects us to go through it. It is hard to go through a closed door. Now that is a true statement, isn't it? God opened doors for our ministry, and although it was not always easy, he expected us to fulfill his will and to make an impact for him.

There would be many opportunities, open doors, for doctors, nurses, dentists, and so many other professionals to make a difference to show God's love to people who had so little of this world's goods. Some of the adversaries I have encountered over the years have often tried to discourage me from continuing into some other area. It might have been a trip into the mountains that would have been difficult even for someone who was used to these sorts of things. I always attempted to get to those who needed our services the most. If there is any scripture in the Bible I believe would be the theme of why we went into this area of Panama, it was the scripture "God has opened a door for me." One of the greatest doors God opened unto this ministry was found in the person of Elena Pimentel.

THIS MAN IS DYING

We arrived in Torti, Panama, late one evening to prepare for a clinic in the Kuna Village of Ipeti. This would be the beginning of a long and fruitful relationship, although it was challenging at times. We were all very tired due to the rough ride over fifty miles of very bad dirt road. It was the first trip down the road for everyone but yours truly. This is part of the tropical vacation that stands out in everyone's mind, their first trip to paradise traveling down the Pan-American Highway. Only God knew just how it was about to get. Our bodies literally tingled as we got out of our two 4×4 SUVs. Everyone was stretching as they looked around at what would be in the future a place all would fall in love with and return to many times. The mountains to the west were beautiful for Torti nestled in a valley surrounded by mountains. It was a hot and muggy day in mid-June. As we stood there in this beautiful setting, we listened to the monkeys in the distance and the many birds as they sang their songs. The roosters were crowing, which was always a joke among us gringos. The roosters were our wakeup call beginning at 4 a.m. In this part of Panama, people travel from all over the world to bird-watch. It is truly an extraordinary place. I believe it is one of the most beautiful places in Panama. I would find myself, as well as many other groups, returning here many times. Perhaps even more extraordinary are the people. Over the next years, many people from this area would become very special to this mission and bring about great changes in our lives.

My life began to take on a whole different meaning. As we unloaded our vehicles, none of us knew how the events of the next several hours were going to affect our lives, and we also were going to see God at work in every one of us.

Being in the middle of the rainy season, the tropics was very hot and muggy. We sat out front of the hotel, discussing how beautiful the surroundings were and waving at the locals as they walked by. We named the hotel the Torti Hilton. This hotel would occupy a great part of this ministry over the next two decades until another hotel was built, which had hot water.

We had been to the local clinic where we dropped off our medicines for safety and also to prepare for the next day. The people of the surrounding communities knew a North American medical team would be working in the local clinic the following day. Dr. Rob Andrews, an emergency medicine doctor from Clay County, Alabama, would be leading the medical team. There also was Vicki Rolling, a registered nurse from Luverne, Alabama, as well as Dr. Jerry Galloway, a dentist from Geneva, Alabama, with his wife, Joy, a registered nurse who would assist him. We also had two ministers, Richard Sport from Greenville, Alabama, and Jimmy Matthews from Troy, Alabama. Jimmy was a tremendous asset to the group due to the fact that he was the only one who spoke Spanish and was able to help in these very difficult times. I was just learning Spanish and knew only how to order some food; however, with my first attempt at a local restaurant, thinking I was ordering rice, I actually ordered women's underwear because I said it wrong. I wondered why the waitress looked funny at me and then started laughing when she said something to another lady. Then she started laughing. I asked what I had said that was so funny. That is when I was informed that they did not sell women's underwear. It took me a long time to live that one down. However, I suppose that's another story.

It was hot, so we all decided to go to bed early. Inside our rooms with no fans, the heat became almost unbearable. Someone asked me what the candle was for; it was on a small table next to the bed. At 10:00 p.m., we found out when they cut the electricity in the community. This was done to save diesel for the community's small diesel generator.

I had just dozed off when a knock came on my door. I was reluctant to open my door for obvious reasons. As I said, my Spanish was only a few words, and I had no clue what the voice on the other side was saying. I finally recognized the voice of the hotel manager and opened the door. He was standing there with a young couple in their early twenties. I learned they were husband and wife. She was crying, and he was, it seemed to me, suffering from a cold. I noticed he was very congested and itching badly. I told them they needed to come to the clinic the next day at 8:00 a.m. He was frantic, so I called Vicki Rolling, who was in the room next to mine. She said we should give him some Benadryl for the itching because it seemed like an allergy. After this, I tried to explain that they could come the next day for a visit with the doctor, but by this time, the young man was on the floor, having problems breathing. Joy Galloway hears the commotion and comes to find out what is going on. She returns to her room for her blood pressure cuff and returns with her husband, who asks, "What's going on out here?" He had the unique ability to make people laugh; however, we were not laughing at this point. We were trying to decide if we needed to wake Dr. Andrews. However, after Joy checked his blood pressure, finding it was 80/60 I run to his room and tell him he is needed. He replied, "Is it one of our people?" It never crossed his mind that it might be a local. I said, "No, but he is in bad shape." He rushes out of his room, and after learning the man's blood pressure was 80/60 and dropping, he says, "This man is dying." And he rushes back to his room, returning with a small vial of medicine. I was to have a lesson in emergency medicine this night. The medicine was epinephrine, a drug that some consider almost a miracle drug. Dr. Andrews is standing there, holding the vial of medicine with a shocked look on his face, saying, "I have the medicine but no way to dispense it." What he needed was a syringe, and the clinic was ten minutes away, and there was no one there this late at night. Vicki Rolling very quickly said, "When we were unpacking our medicines today, I put this syringe in my belly pack. I thought we just might need it." She later related to us while unpacking that she had no idea why she thought she might need the syringe for what purpose would it have without injectable medicine. The story gets even more interesting when Dr. Andrews told us he had decided to pick up a vial of epinephrine at the pharmacy. He thought he might just need it.

He quickly fills the syringe and gives an injection to this young man. His wife at this time is in a panic. We later found out why. In just a few minutes, he begins to respond, and in another few minutes, he is sitting up. He is given another injection and is put up at the hotel so he could be monitored throughout the night. His wife told us he is allergic to penicillin but took it anyway, thinking he would be okay this one time.

I again remember the words of Jesus as he was about to go to the tomb of Lazarus, "The glory of God will be demonstrated here today." How could everything that happened be coincidence? We were in Torti, there was an emergency medicine doctor, the epinephrine and the syringe—all the right things needed to save this young man's life. It was not long until the story was all over town. It seemed everyone knew this young man. God works in ways we cannot even fathom, as he did here. God's glory was truly demonstrated through the lives of us all.

I HAVE NOT SEEN SUCH A GREAT FAITH

She was sitting in the back of the church building as I entered. Someone came to me and said, "Elena has been bitten by a snake." They did not say what kind of snake, and I did not think to ask. As we talked, I found out it was a coral snake, a snake to be feared! I am told it depends where one is bitten on whether they survive or not. She was about fifty miles from the closest doctor or hospital where she could receive treatment. She knew it was not much chance she would be able to survive such a bite. She told me she went to the best place she could have gone in just such a situation—church.

The year was 1997. The place was Torti, Panama! We were conducting a medical campaign to the west in the community of Platanillia, This is a small community with no electricity or any other modern conveniences. It was nestled back in the mountains and was extraordinarily beautiful. This was the second time we had done this kind of work and were fast finding out how difficult this kind of ministry is. On sight was a nurse, Joy Galloway, her husband, Jerry, a dentist from Geneva, Alabama, as well as other medical personnel. There seemed to be no end to the amount of patients this day. We woke up on Sunday morning to a large crowd gathered outside the school where our team had set up a clinic including an improvised dental clinic. This consisted of an old desk for a dental chair and a fire built outside to boil dental instruments. A local was assigned the job of keeping the fire going while Andy Braswell, an electronics specialist from Geneva, Alabama, and close friend of Dr. Galloway, boiled the instruments.

Today was going to be a busy and exciting day. I could tell it by the amount of people lined up to see our doctors. Little did any of us know just how exciting it was about to get. Each person going about his or her duties did not know how their lives would be changed over the next several hours.

While all this was going on, an older gentleman from Greenville, Alabama, Ed Bargainer, commenced to handing out Bible tracts, walking around, smiling at everyone because he knew not one word of Spanish. He would look at a person and give them that big smile and start talking to them all though they did not understand one word he said, but they smiled and took the tract. I always tell people that the smile is universal, a language that all understand. The smile of kindness makes one feel better and says "This person cares about me."

Dr. Galloway decided to take a break to get a breath of fresh air. As he walked out of the classroom, he noticed Ed about to step on a small snake and screamed, "Snake, snake." Jerry, like me, was horrified of snakes. This seemed to be one of his biggest fears in traveling in the tropics. Ed jumps back while an older man armed with a machete chopped down on the snake, killing it. Upon closer examination by the locals, it was determined to be an fer-de-lance or equis snake or for short and x snake. They began to say, "Bad, bad."

It was around 9:00 on Sunday morning when I decided to leave and travel to Torti, ten miles to the east, to get the elements for Communion. We had planned to go around eleven, but for some reason I have never been able to determine, I went up to Cristobal Echavarria, a minister from Panama City, telling him perhaps we should go right away. He asked me what the big hurry was. I replied, "I don't know, but let's go now." The road was in really bad condition, and I could not drive very fast. There were no bridges, and all the small streams, three in number, had to be forded. Being in a 4×4, we had no trouble. We made the trip in about forty-five minutes, arriving at the Torti Church of Christ around 10:45 a.m. People were milling around outside, and some were running back inside. We did not know what was going on. As I pulled up in front of the building, someone runs to the car, screaming, "Elena has been bitten by a snake." I did not know who Elena was and neither did Cristobal. Neither one of us knew at that time how this individual would touch so many lives and change the course of this ministry. This single event changed everything for many years to come. I ran into the building along with Cristobal. Elena was sitting there as though nothing had happened. She even had a smile for me as I touched her shoulder. Cristobal and I both were dumbfounded. We were at a loss for words. Cristobal translated for me as I questioned her as to the kind of snake. I knew little of snakes other than those in Alabama and was scared of all snakes. Neither did I have any medical training. I just tried to be calm like she was. Her husband, Manuel was standing there visibly upset thinking Elena was going to die. With him was their four small children gathered around their mother. He takes his hand and makes a motion like one is cutting something with a knife. It was determined to be the feared coral snake, a snake that is so poisonous most do not survive unless they get to the doctor very quickly.

A coral snake has small teeth, I am told, and cannot strike as other type of snakes with fangs. They must bite a place where the flesh is thin, like between the toes, and then chew, thus dispensing the venom. The snake that had bitten Elena latched on to her between her big toe and the next toe to it and held on. I asked Elena where she was when she was bitten. She, along with her husband and children, lived a four-hour walk from Torti in the mountains in a small thatched hut in a place called Rio

Sereno. The closest church was Torti. As they neared Torti, she stepped on something she thought was a stick, and it rolled under her foot.

She then felt a sharp pain in her foot. Looking down, she saw a multicolored snake hanging on her foot. She pins the snake to the ground and motions for the children to get away, and when they were well away, she shook the snake from her foot and proceeded on to the church building. She said, "I knew I was in big trouble but had a lot of concern for the safety of my children."

Have you ever heard the words "Red and yellow will kill a fellow! Red on black, okay, Jack!" That is the description used in times past to describe the deadly coral snake or one that looks like it that is not poisonous. As a matter of fact, in times past, when a person would be bitten by this type of snake, nothing would even be done other than to try and make the individual a little more comfortable.

We all remember the words of Jesus when an individual had brought their very ill child and let her down in the middle of the roof so Jesus might heal her. The words of the Lord were "I have not seen such a great faith." I personally have never seen such great faith exercised, and it would do much over the years to encourage many people who traveled to Panama. Many people got to know this family and learned from their great faith. Several years later, I decided I would travel to where they lived so I might be able to know and to see for my own eyes what they had to do every Sunday just to come to church. We started out at six o'clock in the morning, traveling into the mountains for hours before finally arriving at their hut. I was so exhausted all I could do was lie in the hammock while my sons and the others went down to the waterfall and jumped in. I could see why they loved this area so much. It was so beautiful, nestled back in the mountains. Elena had captured two chickens on the way up and proceeded making chicken soup for lunch. It was a wonderful visit, and as we returned, finally reaching our four-wheel-drive truck, one individual said, "Now you see what kind of faith these people have."

This book is about people that have exemplified faith, about how God has worked in the lives of others, and above all, about how God works in our own lives if we will allow him to use us. Suffice it to say, each one of us can learn from those who have had their faith tested, which in turn will strengthen our faith.

Those of us who were on this mission trip have always wondered why God put a young Panamanian doctor from Santa Fe, Darién, with us and two medical technicians. We were quick to learn that God knows better than us for none of our nurses or medical people had ever treated snakebite, especially a neurotoxic snakebite. I'm told it does not get worse than this.

We took Elena and put her in our four-wheel drive to rush her back to our medical team. I looked down at my gas gauge and noticed I was almost empty. What a time to be low on gas, I thought. I had no choice, so very quickly, I pulled into the local gas station to get a few dollars' worth of gas. I drove very fast over a very bad road, faster than I should have been driving, but I had no choice. Elena was sick and was perhaps dying. I did not know how God was going to work over the course of the next eight hours. It never dawned on me that I might be taking her to her death, that I should've been driving back west to the closest hospital that would have antivenom, that her chance of survival would be greater if I could just get her to a large hospital where they treated snakebite. I only thought that I must get her to a doctor, and the closest doctor was our medical team. As I continued to drive, Elena became very nauseous, so I stopped so she could vomit. She complained that her head was hurting very badly, but there was nothing I could do but continue to drive. We arrived in about twenty-five minutes to the location of our medical team. We carried her into the school and lay her down on a makeshift bed on the floor. I did not know what else I could do, and all we could do was pray that God would heal her. I knew God would need to intervene in her life in order for her to survive. Joy Galloway ran into the room to make an evaluation of what needed to be done. All of a sudden, everything comes to a halt for everybody now is concentrating on saving the life of this young mother. The Panamanian doctor enters and very quickly evaluates the situation and speaks to the med tech that came with her. He departs running. I did not give any more thought until I saw him running back and sweating profusely. We handed him a bottle of water as he hands something to the doctor.

I learned on this day the power of God and the power of prayer. There were many prayers being offered on behalf of Elena. Everything was working against her from the very beginning, yet perhaps none of us ever realized what her faith would mean on this day. God's power is beyond our imagination, and God will work in the lives of people, and those same people will later become some of his most powerful instruments in his service. I believe it was her faith that saved her life. Yes, there were many other things that came into play, but God used this instance to change the lives of every person there. There was no *earthly* reason I could find why this young woman should live. Everything was against her. She was bitten by one of the most poisonous snakes in Panama. There was no antivenom. She was a long ways from the closest hospital that had any. Yes, everything was against her living with the exception of the power of God. I know there are those who say that this was just a coincidence. I do not believe this because before my own eyes, I saw God in everything. Yes, this changed the course of my ministry in Panama. It changed the lives of everyone, and now, we are all different, having learned from this young woman the power of faith.

She later relates to me, "I was not afraid because I knew I was going to heaven. I was just concerned about my children."

The doctor takes the vial from the hands of the med tech and begins to shake it. She asked then for some sodium chloride. She said she needed 50 cc of sodium chloride. We all looked at one another and said to her, "We do not have anything like that." Joy Galloway looks at me and says, "You didn't bring anything?" I said, "I don't know what's in my luggage." There was a small box when I left Montgomery I could not put on the airplane. I told Betsy, who was not traveling on this trip, just to take it back home because the airlines said I could not take it. I then remembered telling my Betsy, "Just give me the box." I took the things in the box and spread them out in my suitcase. They were samples of medical supplies that had been donated to us. I thought I would take them to Panama and let the doctors there look at them, and maybe they could use them. If they wanted them, there was a lot more in our warehouse and we would ship on the next container.

Joy runs into the room where all of our luggage was and begins to tear through my suitcase, and she screams out, "Here it is!" There were two bags of sodium chloride, 50 cc bags just as the doctor had ordered. She runs back to where Elena lay. Taking the antivenom, she begins to mix it in the sodium chloride. Then the doctor says, "Is there any IV plumbing?" Our hearts dropped because we had left all of that in the clinic "in Torti." There was no time to return to Torti for Elena's health was going downhill. At this point, she was very ill. The nurses and doctors immediately began to rig up a needle, which they injected into her artery, and another needle was used to inject the sodium chloride. A nurse stayed by her side, slowly pushing the plunger and refilling the needle as it ran out. All day long, this process continued. Within two hours, she began to respond favorably, asking for something to drink. Everyone knew that, as a group, we had saved the life of this young woman. However, I do not believe that we should take the credit due to the fact that it seemed every single thing that we needed was made available to the team. Was it simply coincidence, or was each one of us who witnessed this event, the saving of the life of this beautiful young mother, simply part of a greater plan?

By late evening, we were able to return her to her husband and children, who were still anxiously waiting close to the church building for her return. There was extreme elation when we pulled up and she got out of the vehicle. God truly worked in the lives of us all on this day, causing each one of us to use our talents.

This is a part of the speech that Elena gave at our 2009 Friends of Panama Mission's Dinner, giving account of the snakebite.

> I live in a place called Rio Sereno, which is a long way in the mountains, about a three-hour walk, and sometimes we ride a horse. My daughter Yoice would walk about one hour to school. We also would walk to Torti to church. We had a lot of difficulties in our life but never compared with Jesus. My husband, Jose Manuel, would work with the machete for five dollars a day. There was never enough money, but we were happy, and we gave God our heart. One day, we were traveling to Torti with my baby and my daughter, who was on the horse. I was leading the horse, and I felt something bite me as it rolled under my foot. I was thinking it was a small plant that had a needle, but when I see my foot, I saw a small snake running from my foot. I saw it bite me on my toe, and then I saw two small drops of blood. I cleaned the blood off my foot and continued walking. I went on to church for it was morning. I was beginning to feel very bad, and then I tell one of the brothers of the church a snake bit me. In that moment, Larry Brady, who was with a medical team in Platanillia, drives up in a car. He found out how bad I was then takes to the medical team. I am very sick and vomit, and my head is hurting very bad. They began to give me medicine intravenously with a small needle. Everyone was very worried and said I would probably die but, God had a plan for me. Because of what happened to me, perhaps many

people have received help, and perhaps now all could see the necessity of this work in Panama. Because of Panama Missions, many people are helped and receive benefit like my sisters in Christ Daryelis, Omaira, and Anayansi, and so many other people that have benefited from eye surgery, houses and cement floors, wheelchairs and glasses, and so many other things. I know all of this because if the snake had not bitten me, I would not know about this mission work. This is why I say the snakebite was a blessing and not a curse.

Elena Pimentel, Torti, Panama

Several years after this event, Elena became very ill again. We sent her to Panama City, where she underwent a lot of tests, but the tests were not conclusive and an improper diagnosis was given. Some thought she might have lupus while others thought she might have fibromyalgia along with other illnesses. She became so ill she was almost unable to function; therefore, we sent her to a private hospital in Panama City, where a battery of tests were done. None of us, including Elena and all the medical people that had been to Panama with us, would have ever suspected the final diagnosis. Elena was diagnosed with a form of leprosy. I went immediately to see her, and she began to cry uncontrollably. She said to the me, "I am not afraid to die. I have only concern for my children." This type of leprosy is very rare, and we were told it is usually found in Mexico. The doctors asked her if she had been to Mexico. She said, "No, never." The antivenom she had taken years earlier is thought to have been the problem. This form of leprosy, according to the doctor in Panama City and from the CDC in Atlanta, is 100 percent curable with the proper antibiotics. It takes a period of two years for the right kind of antibiotics to clear the individual of leprosy. After a period of two years of taking antibiotics, Elena is cured of this terrible disease.

MY NAME IS DANELY

She was standing there in front of a church building in southwestern Panama, barefooted, holding her small sister on her hip. I was curious to find out who she was and where she lived. I went over to her and said, "Hello, how are you? What is your name?" She replied, "My name is Danely." I thought to myself, *She is just a child who must take on adult responsibilities.*

Every time I returned to this town, she was always there—another year older, a little prettier, but still looking as though she were an adult. One year as I was about to leave Torti, I learned that Danely had graduated from the ninth grade and, being a good student, would like to go on to the next level, which we would call the tenth grade. In order for this to happen, she would have to go to the next largest town where there was a high school, which was either Chepo or Panama City. I was completely taken with her because I had raised five sons and felt it would be nice to have a daughter. After making arrangements to live with a family in Panama City, she enrolled in a private school to continue her studies. After she graduated from high school, we told her, with no promises, that if she could learn English enough to pass the TOEFL (an English test) to qualify for attending a university in the United States, we would make every effort for her to study in Alabama. She knew no English, and with 100 percent commitment and with our help financially, she learned English and was accepted to study at Faulkner University in

Montgomery, Alabama. Over the next four years, she studied diligently. It was not easy because of cultural problems and being extremely homesick; however, she overcame all the obstacles. For several months, she lived with my son Jim and his family until she could move into the dorm.

She caught the eye of the people in the Bible department, and to help her overcome some of the obstacles she was facing, like not having spending money for some of the basics a student would need, she was given a job. She worked for all of the professors, helping grade their papers and file their papers for them. She also helped with different aspects of the Bible department under the direction of the dean. Everyone loved her, which made her stay in the United States so much easier.

We watched her walk across the stage to receive her diploma with a degree in psychology. After receiving her diploma on stage, she looked out over the audience, catching our eye with a big smile. She had worked hard and endured much to get to this point. However, it was not just my family who was involved in helping her reach her goal. Dr. and Mrs. Dean Moberly became heavily involved in her life and began paying for her dorm as well as tuition so she could finish. Danely did not let any of us down. She was committed to completing her education. Back in Panama was her boyfriend, Tito Miranda, who wanted to get married, but she, in no uncertain terms, told him that you cannot live on love and he would have to wait until she finished school. I was very proud of her and knew she was going to make everyone proud. She did not let us down.

I've always wondered what she would've become if we had not intervened in her life. A young lady who could not speak a word of English now speaks fluently and helps translate for groups that travel to Panama.

Today, she is married to a fine minister and has a job with Dell Corporation because someone decided not to walk by on the other side of the road. None of us have ever regretted our intervention in Danely's life.

Over the years, our intervention in her life brought about much change in my family because during some of those years, there were times of struggle. We at times tried to justify why we should stop helping her, but each time, we considered the possibilities of her future without us. What would she have become? Where would she be? From my own observation and experience and travels, I know that unless someone got involved in her life, her future did not look good. The best she could expect would be to start having babies at an early age. I have seen it over and over where someone who had so much promise got tired of waiting and moved in with the first person who made them a better offer than that which they were currently in.

Betsy and I learned so much as we watched the transformation of Danely. She changed from a very timid person to someone with great confidence. People at church as well as her professors and the dean, saw the confidence of Danely growing.

Upon returning home for a visit during a break in school, she spoke to a group of young people about their future. What she said was amazing. Her words to these young people were "Close your eyes and then imagine where you will be in five years or ten years." At a party for Panama Missions celebrating 25 years of ministry in Panama different ones spoke about what those years meant to them.

Danely touched us all when she said, "You took a chance on me, and because of that, I have a future." This touched me deeply because it demonstrated all I had been telling people all over the United States. "Get involved and make a difference."

Each one of us can sit on the sidelines and look on and complain about all the bad in the world, or we can become involved and help change the future. The future can be changed for the better but not until each one of us who claims to be a

Christian becomes involved in our church, in our community, and in our world. Let us say "Let us have a better world and let it begin with me." I heard a statement from a preacher many years ago as I was waiting my turn to speak at a lectureship that went like this, and I have never forgotten it: "If everyone was just like me what kind of world would this world be?"

The following are the words of Danely:

> Panama Missions has been a great blessing in my life. Since the moment I started receiving those precious Christmas boxes, my life started to change. I remember at night staring at all the good things inside those boxes. It was wonderful to see the variety of goodies; it felt like I had many, many gifts. They were the only gifts we received for Christmas since my mother could not afford to give my brother and sister and me Christmas or birthday gifts.
>
> My life started to change in a more meaningful way when Panama Missions gave me the opportunity for a future. I had no support and no way to accomplish my dreams. As a little girl, my biggest dream was to become a professional and help my family financially. I was the oldest of my brothers and sisters, and as the oldest, I learned that it is hard to live day by day, economically speaking. We would prepare tamales to sell throughout the community in order to make a little money. I wanted a different future, and my only option was education.
>
> Larry and Betsy Brady of Panama Missions made education possible for me. Thanks to them, I completed my high school and then went on English school to learn English, which allowed me to apply for a scholarship at a university in the United States. I graduated from Faulkner University in Montgomery, Alabama, and have now returned to Panama. I now work for a large company and have recently been promoted.
>
> I am so thankful for Larry Brady for believing in me and my potential. I now am the professional I always

dreamed about. There also was another family, Dr. Dean and Dorothy Moberly, who helped pay for much of my tuition and so many other things I needed while in college. Because of all the help and encouragement I have received from so many people, I am now happily married and living the future I dreamed about when I was a little girl. I cannot imagine how my life would have been if Panama Missions would have not come to change my life.

Danely Cardenas Miranda

WE CAN DO THAT

A few years ago, I was in Panama on a mission trip. I received a call from Tom Ford, president of the Gift of Life Foundation. He told me about a man who had established an organization called the Wheelchair Foundation. He was wealthy; as a matter of fact, he was, according to his book, *Road to Purpose*, listed in *Forbes Magazine* as one of the four hundred richest men in America. This man owned mansions, hundreds of classic cars, a jet plane, and his own football team, but there was something missing in his life. On a trip to Vietnam, he visited a small village outside of Hanoi. What happened next changed the course of his life. A little girl, six years old, had never moved by herself. She sat there, he said, terrified and crying on an old pile of rags. He said he gave her some lollipops, but that didn't help very much, and then he took her outside and put her in a wheelchair. She was frightened and tearful as he showed her how to put her hands on the wheel rims to move the wheelchair. She was finally able to move it by herself, then she broke out into the biggest smile he had ever seen. All the people clapped and cheered. In a few moments, they had transformed this girl from a pile of rags into a girl who could move about freely. The wheelchair had opened up a new life for her. She now can go to school and build a future. She has found a new world. This man's name was Kenneth Behring. What he did on that day changed the course of his life. He has now given out tens of thousands of wheelchairs around the world. (Used by permission Road to Purpose Kenneth Behring Blackhawk Press http://www.wheelchairfoundation.org) He found a ministry by touching the life of someone so small. I am sure Mr. Behring would tell you and me that it does not take a rich person to touch a life—to make a difference.

I had breakfast with him and his son David, and we each talked about the passion of helping others, each one in his own way but making a difference. In the end, we reached the same conclusion—in every life we touched, we got back more than we gave.

Throughout this book, I write about how everyone should have a ministry such as the one Mr. Behring found. I am sure it did not come the way he thought it would. So many search but never find what they are looking for. Perhaps they are looking in all the wrong places and with the wrong motives.

Even before I met Mr. Behring, I had introduced my mother to a set of twins in Torti, Panama, not by her traveling there but by a picture I had taken of these girls standing outside the shack where they lived. Mom was moved by these two little girls and their poverty. She decided very quickly something had to be done, but she had little money; therefore, she was limited by what she could do. One day, she was sitting in her small apartment, making a blanket for one of her many grandchildren. It dawned on her what she could do. She could make them some clothes from material she already had. Calling me, she asked me to find out what size clothes they wore, and with that information, she got her sewing machine and went to work. The results—two identical dresses, and then she made some more dresses for another child who lived in the same community, a young lady by the name of Yoice Pementel. When mom was eighty-four years old, she made her first trip to Panama with me. Our first stop was the shack where the twins lived with their parents. You should have seen the smiles of these girls as they received their first brand-new dresses. The dresses were identical, and Mom helped them change into their new dresses. They were so proud of their new dresses. Mom returned to the United States a different person, determined to do something for others—to help some of those people she had met on this trip. Again, she got out her sewing machine and started sewing. She was living in a retirement center on the campus of Faulkner University in Montgomery, Alabama. An elderly neighbor asked her what she was doing. She replied, "I'm making dresses for little girls in Panama," showing this lady what she was doing. Getting out the album, they looked at the pictures of twin girls receiving their dresses. The impact was unexpected. The lady said, "I can do that." So she gets out her sewing machine and begins to make dresses. When other ladies from their church heard what they were doing, they all began to say, "We can do that." They began to make dresses. It began to catch on as other churches around the United States heard what was going on. Now, senior citizens who have had no ministry, who did not know they could be part of a mission team without even leaving their house, are making a difference. In Arkansas in 2010, a ninety-two-year-old Christian lady made over three hundred dresses for the children of Panama. Now, they're coming in from everywhere because so many have found some way to serve they did not even know existed.

"What can I do?" you might ask. And I would say to you, "You are not too young and you're not too old to learn how to serve." There is something for everyone to do, and it does not cost a lot of money.

Panama Mission's Operation Christmas Joy program began with three bags of toys for the children's hospital in the Republic of Panama and now has over seven thousand Christmas gifts and Christmas bags each year. It has opened up a new ministry for hundreds of people both young and old to make a difference in the lives of someone somewhere who will not receive a Christmas gift.

We are not changed by power or money but by simple people, people who had nothing to give me back. My motto is, "Help someone who cannot pay you back." We get the greatest reward when we understand this principle of not always wanting something in return. I have been taught this in more ways than one as I have developed this ministry over the years.

In December of 2010, there was severe flooding throughout Panama, and four of us were stranded on the Darién side of Panama, unable to travel to Panama City. We were told it would be approximately three or four days before we would be able to travel back to Panama City. So we just hunkered down, so to speak, in Torti. We were really not in any form of danger other than the fact that the community was quickly running out of food and bottled water as well as fuel, which would mean no power because the generator runs on diesel. There were also Peace Corps workers who needed to get out of the community and were waiting for word of when that might happen. We got word that we would be departing for Panama City and could only take our backpack for obvious reasons. The Panamanian government sent a bus to pick us up and take us to the water's edge and then transported us by boat to the other side of the lake. As we climbed out of the boat next to a cemetery, there were photographers from local newspapers taking pictures. We appeared on the front page of the newspapers, us gringos from North America stranded in Panama floods. The government had brought a big dump truck for people to get in. I do not believe much thought had gone into how people were supposed to get into the back of the truck and then get out at the other end. The truck body was higher than my head and would even be a struggle for me to get in. Betsy just stands there and looks at the truck and then says, "How in the world are we supposed to get up in that truck?" This was not only my wife's sentiment but others as well. Betsy had already made up her mind she was not even going to try. If she had to she would walk to where we were to catch a bus.

There was a man standing over to the side next to an old beat-up pickup truck. It looked like it had been to a demolition derby. We were approached by this rather tall Panamanian who was the driver of the truck. He said, "My name is Jesus." He told us he would take us in his truck to where we could get transportation back into the city. As we were getting into the truck, he said, "Do not try to pay me anything for this is something I want to do." This man had a great desire to provide a service, and it was something he could do, and he expected nothing in return. I could tell just by talking to him that it really made him feel good to provide this service. We could look at him and know he was not an individual who made a lot of money. However, in our discussions as we rode along, one could tell that this man loved his faith. As we rode along we all noticed his humility and with a name like Jesus he was exemplifying the life of Christ by his service. He had the resources, which was an old truck, to get us to where we needed to be.

We have so many material blessings and it is important for us to always learn to share that which we have and expect nothing back. God's people usually always share what they have even if it is small. But in the words of an old Indian chief, "Small for you but big for us." It brings about a great source of satisfaction knowing you did something for someone even to relieve the anxiety they are feeling due to certain circumstances beyond their control.

A part of missionary work I have always enjoyed is visiting the local people in their houses enjoying their hospitality for they like to share what they have. As I sat there I looked around and wondered how it came to all of this, that is, my being here on the bank of this river, sitting here in this hut with these sweet people who had no television or telephone, no running water or bathroom facilities, but they were smiling and were so happy I was sitting here in their house. She was such a small woman, and her husband was maybe a head taller and had a big smile on his face. She had no fancy clothes, just a wraparound that was typical of their culture. Sitting there, I felt, this is where I need to be. They were so happy for me to be in their home, and they want nothing in return. She busied herself around the fire, cooking what I learned was a piece of alligator. I wondered if I was going to have to sample the alligator meat, which I would have had it been offered to me. I suppose I considered myself lucky to have departed before it was fully cooked. I've often wondered what it would've tasted like. She had a pot of rice sitting on the logs, cooking. They would take three small logs and put the ends of the logs together and put the fire in the middle, and as the logs burned, they would push them and keep the ends together, thus the pot would sit on those logs as she cooked. I found myself liking the simple surroundings and the peacefulness that I felt. She gives me a great big smile and says in Spanish, "You want some coffee?" I love coffee and knew anything boiled long enough would not make me sick, so I made a big deal about how much I would enjoy a cup of coffee. I did not know it had been sitting there all day, and she added some water from the river with a little more coffee and more sugar. With a big smile upon her face, she hands me and Manuel Pimentel a cup and watches as I take a sip. I almost gagged but maintained a straight face. It was the worse concoction anyone had every called coffee. Manuel asked me how I liked my coffee. Neither one of us could dump it because she was watching, never losing the big ear-to-ear smile she had. I just smiled back and took another sip. I managed to drink most of it, and I am glad I did for we have such a close relationship that has caused us to love each another. I always return for a visit when I am in the area but swore off asking for coffee.

It is so vital for us to put aside our comforts for a time to let people know they are loved.

An important lesson to all who desire to do any kind of missionary work is this: you cannot build relationships in a hotel room. You must get out there with the people. The Bible talks about God opening doors for us. To try to make my point, I always say that it would be good if the door God opened for us was next to the road, no struggles, no difficulty, no walking, and no sweating. You could just get out of the car and walk through the door. We have to get out of our comfort zone and visit in their homes and enjoy their hospitality, allowing them to teach us. I am convinced that it is not always all the big things but so many small things that really do make a difference in the lives of others and, perhaps more importantly, in our own lives.

THE BLIND SEE

In Torti, Panama, a makeshift eye clinic had been set up in a local school. People could come in and have their eyes checked and, if needed, have cataract surgery. As always, the lines were long for the poor did not have the money to pay for this surgery. A very small lady approaching eighty years old, according to her daughter, came to be seen. She had been totally blind for seven years. After she was evaluated, it was determined she was a candidate for surgery. Her daughter was elated, and that is putting it mildly. After going through all the tests, she was led into the operating room to be prepared for surgery. She was having a difficult time keeping her eye still, so she had to receive a very painful injection, which the doctors do not like to give, but in her case, it was needed in order to complete the operation. The surgery lasted about twenty-five minutes and was very successful. She asked the doctor if he would operate on her other eye. Normally, they only do one eye because so many are waiting, but in this case, they could not refuse. She returned the following day for postop and to be prepared for surgery on the second eye. After surgery, she was taken home by her daughter and returned the following day to have the bandage removed. Sitting there after the removal of her bandage, she was able to see very clearly from both eyes. Her daughter fell to her knees and, with hands reaching into the air, started praising God. Her mother repeatedly said over and over, "Oh glory, *Dios*." Continuing to chant the name of God as her daughter, on her knees in front of her mother, continued to cry, not believing what she was witnessing. She was moved outside so the doctor could determine how good she could see. In all of this, she ceased not praising God for her new lease on life. She was asked to look out and tell what she saw. She says, "I see the tree, and a bird is in the tree. I see the road, and there goes a car down the road." A crowd had gathered, witnessing what they said was a miracle. To all these people, it was nothing short of a miracle. People were milling around, talking about what they had just witnessed—the blind receiving sight.

The following year we decided to bring the eye surgery team to Meteti, a small town located on the Panama American Highway about 150 miles southeast of Panama City. The team consisted of four surgeons and a general medical team with a dentist. We had never worked in this part of Panama. As one travels in this direction, you get closer to the border to Columbia. This often causes a lot of fear due to problems in times past with rebel groups. There had not been any problems for several years. Our operations were set up in the local medical clinic. It was quickly converted into a first-class operating room with very modern equipment. The locals were amazed at the transformation of their clinic and would become even more amazed as people came into the clinic blind and would leave with their sight. On the first day, the lines were extremely long with so many blind people. Dr. Russ Burcham, an ophthalmologist from Denver, Colorado, said, "I believe I now know how Jesus must have felt when he saw the crowds." One can become overwhelmed very quickly when the crowds begin to push and shove, hoping they would be selected for surgery.

This week's mission would again center upon an individual who would completely steal the hearts of everyone present, both North American and Panamanian. Who would have ever thought that God's glory would be demonstrated through this individual? She came in being led by her parents. It did not take one very long to see that this child was blind. They first saw Dr. Sally Scott, who immediately referred her to Dr. Burcham. She said she decided he needed to make the decision whether she would be a candidate for surgery. I do not know if it ever crossed his mind if he should operate. She had cataracts on both eyes. She was only ten years old. Her mother said she went blind at the age of three, and being from the mountains, there was no money for this type of surgery. I personally had never heard of a child having cataracts. I learned there is what is called congenital cataracts, which means she was born with them. The surgery was scheduled immediately. I watched with her parents as she was taken into the pre-op room and prepared for surgery. Her mother started crying because this was all foreign to them. I thought to myself, how frightening this must be for people who lived in the mountains. The next time they saw her was about an hour later when she was led out of the room with a patch over her eye. No one would know until the following day if the surgery was successful. The next morning, I was sitting at an outdoor restaurant, drinking coffee. This little girl was sitting at the next table, eating a piece of chicken. She had her patch on, waiting for her post-op appointment with Dr. Burcham. When they departed, I followed them into the clinic and watched as the patch was removed. She could see for the first time since she turned three. She looked at her mother, who was crying, and smiled. She smiled at everyone. She then did something no one was expecting—not even her mother. She looked at Dr. Burcham and, speaking directly to him, she asked, "Will you operate on my other eye?" How could he say no? She was so young and had her whole life ahead of her. She was scheduled for surgery the following day. When she arrived the following day, there was a reporter from the *La Prensa*, a newspaper from Panama, who interviewed the mother, who said, "I have no words to express how I feel. We will wait until tomorrow to see if this surgery is a success." The next day, Thursday, the day the team departs for a few days of rest and recreation after a very busy week, she comes in with both parents for post-op. This time, all the ones who worked with her were there, including the reporter. The patch is removed, and Dr. Burcham looks into the eye to see if all looks okay and then holds up his four fingers, asking, How many? She says, "Four." He says, "Great!" He then has her turn and look down the hall and says, "Now tell me what you see." She says, Everything! There was not a dry eye in the house, including the reporter's. A new lease on life was given to this beautiful ten-year-old girl. Money cannot buy this kind of happiness we witnessed this day, and to think that so many had a small part on such a success story. We cannot perform miracles as Jesus did, but to these people, a miracle was preformed this day. I often think of this little girl and all who made it possible to be one of the success stories of this mission.

PAPA LARRY IS COMING

I was sitting in the house of an Embera family I had met several years earlier, Demas and Elena Chami. I would sometimes stop by and enjoy a meal with them if I happen to be in the area. They lived about eight feet off the ground, which was typical of the Embera Indians and always fascinated me. They were a wonderful family who would become such a vital part of this ministry. Demas had chased a rabbit down and grilled the meat while Elena prepared some rice. It was a meager meal, but they wanted to share it with me, so I ate it. It was hard for me to get used to eating rice with nothing in it, not even salt. It did not taste bad, just bland. They had so little to share but always shared what they had with me. It made them happy that I would sit in their house. She said to me, "My house is not beautiful." My reply was, "Your house is your heart, and you have a beautiful heart." This family was my first encounter with the Embera people, who I would come to love and have a great admiration.

I was visiting in their home one day when I noticed a baby in a small box not much bigger than a shoe box. She was eight days old. As I stood there with this small baby in my arms, little did I know how she would affect me and how I would come to love her as I watched her grow up. If she continued in the village, she was in for a hard life because life among the Embera is a rough life. This one little girl would melt the heart of all who would encounter her charm. I became Papa Larry to her. Her mom said she would wait for me, thinking I should come more often. One day, as she was outside, she saw an airplane fly over and said, "Papa Larry is coming." When I did not show up in a few hours, she started crying. What a special child she has become.

As Yati began to grow, I found myself having a difficult time staying away from her village, and even though I was not to be in that area, I would make every effort to go visit. She was always waiting as though she knew Papa Larry would come today. I always had some small gift and tried to give her family a little money to help out in difficult times.

One day, I arrived in the village and found out that her mother had been working very hard on a basket that was extraordinary in its beauty. She was not quite through with the basket and said she would have it ready when I returned from a visit to the Darién for the road passed by their village. Upon my return several days later, she presented me with this basket, which I cherish. I remember this small child smiling up at me and her mother sitting there with this work of art. The basket has crosses all the way around, and I asked her, "How did you get it so beautiful and so perfect?" Her reply to me was, "I have the picture in my mind."

Everyone who knows Yati has come to love her, but I tell anyone, she's my little girl. She is a product of this ministry. She is very intelligent and one of the most spiritual children for her age I have ever known. She is now twelve years old and beautiful. I asked her what she wanted to be when she grows up. Her answer really did not surprise me when she replied she wanted to be a doctor.

Because of a bad situation in their community, Demas decided to move his family closer to where Yati attended school. This would be in the community of Torti. Taking money he had received from the sale of a small house and piece of land, he purchased a small lot and built a lean-to house on it. It was mostly a shed with some old plastic wrapped around it to keep out the wind and rain. He dug a toilet and made a place to take a shower using water from a bucket. There is no electricity or running water. He worked hard to make it livable for his family, but it was far from comfortable because the floor was dirt, and the mosquitoes were very bad. In June 2011, I arrived with a mission group from the United States. We arrived in the Torti community to begin working and helping where we could. We had decided as part of a service project that we would put a cement floor in the house of this family. At this point, the house was nothing more than a shed in the middle of the field, but as time went on, it began to take on the look of a house although there was no indoor plumbing or electricity, and the floor was mud. After obtaining the cement, gravel, and all that was needed, the team began their work. At the end of the week, when everyone gathered at the house to look at the floor, the father, through his tears, began to thank everyone for their hard work. There was a lot of crying and a lot of happiness because this group had made a difference in the lives of these wonderful people. It does not take a lot to make people happy when one has so little. This is a lesson we all should to learn in the United States of America. God expects us to share that which we have with others. Yati has a bedroom where she can be comfortable and be out of the elements.

It has always been amazing to me how sometimes people just need someone to suggest or show them a need and then they become involved. Just such a case was found in Montgomery, Alabama, of a family who owned a children's furniture store. The furniture in the store were sold to clientele who only wanted the best. There was a beautiful white bed on display that caught my eye. A Christian lady who owned this furniture store said, "I cannot sell this bed because it has a chip on it, so I want to donate it to this little girl, Yati, that you have been telling us about." She was also going to need a mattress, and this mattress set has a small defect, so now I had a full bed with mattresses.

She also was going to need somewhere to store her clothes. There was a matching dresser, and next to it was a side table that was donated because it to was supposed to have a small defect, which we never could find. She was going to need pillows and a comforter and sheets, and before it was over, our little girl, Yati, had a beautiful bedroom including a canopy with a mosquito net, all of this simply because a family was shown something they could do in making a difference in the lives of someone else. All of these items were placed on our container in December and delivered to Yati. Every time people come to visit, they have to go look at Yati's room. When she moved to their new house, her father wrapped up Yati's furniture to protect it. It all looks a little odd sitting there on a mud floor, but after our team poured a concrete floor in her room, they put her bed and all the furniture together. Yati's room is beautiful and was made possible because others cared, people who did not know her, had never met her, and would never meet her unless she was able to travel to the United States, but they came and made a difference in her life.

Over the years, each time I go to Panama, when I spend money, I always have a little change left I put it aside and save, and before I depart Panama, I give it to Yati. One day, when I was visiting in their home, she bought out a can full of the change I had given to her. She was saving it, not spending it. Her mother looked at me and said, "That's Yati's money Papa Larry gave her." It does fill me with humility to know that something so insignificant could bring such change and a grateful heart to someone who needed it so badly.

Yati has been a great teacher for everyone who has come in contact with her. Through her smile, her contentment with her surroundings, her love for her parents, and above all, her love for me, she has taught us all so much. It does not take riches to bring about happiness for this little girl has no riches, but she has always told me, "Papa Larry, I have what I need, and I love you."

Strive to bring change, to bring happiness, to make a difference in someone's life even though it might be little, for when one has so little, a little seems like it's big.

I remember a statement from an old chief who was thanking us for coming to the village. He was saying "Thank you, thank you, thank you." He was beaming with gratitude. I said to him, "It's just a small thing." He said to me, "Little for you, but big for us." I thought about that over the years. It is not all about the big things but about the many small things one does in life.

While in Panama, we had just completed a medical campaign at the Clinic of Hope. I received information to call Yati for she had reached a point in her life where she understood that God was working with her and through her, and she knew it was time for her to become a Christian. The greatest compliment one could ever have is to have someone say "I want you to be a part of my becoming a child of God." And not only that, she wanted Papa Larry to baptize her. I called her and told her I would be coming through Torti on my way to Panama City and I would meet her so I could baptize her. Upon our arrival, she was standing with her parents, waiting for me. We proceeded to a small swimming pool where I watched the beautiful young lady put on Christ. After I baptized her, she began to cry as I hugged her. My mind traveled back over the years to that day twelve years earlier when I first saw this small baby and fell in love with her, and now I see this baby in Christ who is now my sister in Christ.

Panama Missions has a program that allows young people to visit the United States if they meet certain criteria. They must be good students and be referred by their teachers. They must also be of good character, participative in their church, and be recommended by their leadership. It was never a question in my mind that Yati would be one of the children to participate in this program. I almost could not wait until she turned twelve, which is the cutoff age I have established for visiting students. She was selected to travel in the summer of 2012. She was elated although very nervous about leaving her parents and the surroundings that were familiar to her. She told me she had heard so much about the United States but never crossed her mind she would be able to visit such a country. She obtained her passport and then traveled to the US Embassy in Panama City to receive her visa. Those who have traveled to the United States tell me that this is one of the scariest things in the process of preparing to travel. Everything is ready; the day has arrived to travel into Panama City for the flight to United States the following day.

We arrived early at the airport on the morning of June 9, 2012, to check in with Delta Air Lines. Her mother begins to cry and tells me to make sure I take care of her daughter. They have never been separated before, and just being in the airport is a very scary thing for them. Yati is beautiful and has even been painted in their cultural paints on her arms and legs. I could tell she was very nervous but excited. After saying our goodbyes, we pass through immigration and security and arrive at our gate to wait for our plane. It is finally time to board the airplane. She is traveling with another young lady from Sanson, Darién, Neilis Saenz, fifteen years old, who also was totally overwhelmed by what she was experiencing. I personally cannot contain myself and the emotion I was feeling as I watched them walk down the breezeway into the airplane. As they entered the airplane, they just stopped seeing all those people sitting there. We find our seats with Neilis sitting next to the window and Yati in the middle next to my wife and me across the aisle. They were both very afraid, and their hands were sweating for all this was so new. To watch someone begin to experience things we so much take for granted cannot be expressed, I do not believe I can even express in words. It is overwhelming to watch the expression on their faces as they hear the engines begin to accelerate as we begin speeding down the runway for takeoff. The airplane breaks ground, and they are pushed back into their seats, and Yati's mouth flies open for she's looking at the top of the airplane. We tell her to look out the window. She looks out and is totally amazed for now she is looking down at her country. We break through the clouds, and she now feels she is a bird soaring among the clouds. Tears welled up in my eyes, causing me to look away. Her expression and the reaction from doing something she had only heard about is heartwarming. She has seen the planes fly over but never expected to be in one of them.

We finally land after three hours and forty-five minutes of flight time to Atlanta. As we stepped off the plane into the United States, I said to her, "Welcome to the United States."

We stopped at my favorite restaurant, Cracker Barrel for a late lunch of chicken fingers and potatoes with all the trimmings. I just watched as they enjoyed. We finally arrived at our home in Pintlala, Alabama. As we walk through the door, I say, "Welcome, my house is your house." We show her to her bedroom, and she just sits down on the middle of the bed, bouncing up and down. We are all so excited for all the planning and all the efforts for making all this happen has finally come to be a reality. Money does not buy this type of happiness. All the things she was experiencing for the first time in her life brought a great sense of gratification. Things like a first airplane ride, eating pizza, seeing an elephant or simply being pulled on a big tube about the lake and hearing her as she screams with joy.

Dr. Joe Wilhite allowed her to steer his pontoon boat around the lake in Tennessee and drive his golf cart up and down the hills in front of his house. Hearing her laughter as she hit the brakes too hard or accelerate too fast brought a lump into my throat. These are things she had only read about in books and seen on television, and because people cared, she now is able to witness all these things we so much take for granted.

My advice to people is to choose someone who has never experienced the joys of the firsts. Help them fulfill a dream. When you help someone fulfill a dream, a life is changed forever, and you, the individual, will be made better by bringing about that change. Understand me, it is not about money, for most good things are never completed because money gets in the way. If we allow money to always stop us from doing a good work, then we need to start looking at our stewardship.

Yes, my little girl had the experience of a lifetime, an experience she will never forget. One can never know the impact you will have upon others all along life's pathway.

Here are the words of Yati:

> I was born on June 16, 1999, in a small village in the Darién Province of Panama. My mother and father met Larry Brady over twelve years ago. I was only eight days old when one day, Papa Larry came to visit. My parents told me of this visit and how special it was.
>
> Papa Larry has been helping me and my family all of my life. We attended the Church of Christ in Santa Fe, Darién. We lived in this area for four years until one day, some brothers from the church along with Papa Larry built us a house in another community so we could have a better life and I could go to school. We lived here for five years, but my school was a bit far, so my father decided to sell the house and use the money to buy a small piece of land where he built us a house. The house did not have a floor, electricity, or water, but we were happy with what God had done for us. One day, Papa Larry came with a group from the United States who built us a concrete floor. We recently were able to get electricity in our house. Having our house here was so much better because my school is very close. There is a medical clinic as well as police, a grocery store, and other things that we need much closer. My mother and father were so happy because now

it was not so hard for me to go to school, which is located very near to our house.

We now attend church in the community of Platanilla. My family says that now we have found our true family in Christ Jesus.

In the year 2011, Papa Larry started the paperwork for my passport so I can visit the United States. When I was small, Papa Larry asked me if I wanted to go to America with him someday. I said, "Yes, when I am ten years old." I did get to go after I turned thirteen.

I received my visa in April 2012 in order to travel to the United States on June 10, 2012.

I learned so many things I did not understand before. Another thing I have learned is after I was baptized, many blessings have come into my life. First, I will never tire of thanking God for my family and for Papa Larry and his family. I feel they have an important place in my family and I in theirs. Also, for the second time, Panama Missions helped us in the construction of our house, of the floor, and the installation of electricity.

I feel I still have not finished counting all that has been done for us, but what little I can tell, I want to suggest that the person reading realize that God loves you, God loves me, and God loves this world even though it is filled with sin, and while you are in the United States and I in Panama, we have something in common, we are all children of God.

"I can do everything through Christ Jesus who strengthens me" (Philippians 4:13).

With much love,
Yatiza Chami

WHERE THERE IS HOPE THERE IS LIFE

Hope means a "great expectation" or "the happy anticipation of good." I expect something good to happen. A common definition of *hope* is "desire plus expectation." The Bible, in Romans 8:25, says, "But if we hope for that we see not, then do we with patience wait for it."

Perhaps the following story of one family's struggle to come to grips with the tragedy of having two children die in as many years will help us understand how people feel about the United States.

In 2005, I was in Panama in early January, preparing for a medical group. I heard that a young lady I had known since she was a little girl had been admitted to the public hospital in Panama City, Panama, for suffering from severe headaches. The year before, I had received a phone call asking if we could help pay for a scan on this young lady. They thought she was having headaches because of a fall from a horse and was concerned she had received a brain injury. The scan was done; it was determined she had a mass on her brain that had nothing to do with the fall from a horse.

Due to the family not having money, an MRI had not been done. She was six months pregnant, so they were limited on some of the medicine that could be given her for the seizures she was suffering. I immediately went to the hospital to visit her and was met by her father, Chama, and her mother, Derfilia. I had not yet seen Daryelis. I asked how she was doing, and her mother started crying. She was having lots of seizures, and the medicine she was on was caused her great pain when administered through her IV. Also, they were trying to get her far enough along to save the baby if she died.

A year earlier, this same family had suffered the loss of their eighteen-year-old daughter Jennifer in an automobile accident. They were no strangers to tragedy. Her father looks at me with strain in his eyes and says, "Brother, can you take her to the United States? You all have everything there." It struck me like a bolt of lightning: "You have everything there." I have traveled all over the world and have seen a lot of cultures but never gave it a thought that we had everything. He looked at me as though I was his last hope to save his beautiful twenty-two-year-old daughter. His hope was within the borders of the country I call home, the United States of America. I was struck for he did not know that he might be asking the impossible, so I told him I would make some calls and see what we could do but that it would be a long shot. However, the first thing we needed to do was have an MRI done and see what was actually going on. Panama Missions paid for the MRI, and the result was not good. We informed the family the MRI would be sent to different hospitals in the United States hoping a Doctor would at least talk to us but we did not offer them much hope.

I went in to see Daryelis and had an emotional time talking with her. She had the most beautiful smile. My heart wanted to melt. I thought within myself, she is here not knowing if she will live or die, and she smiles and chatters to me like, "I'm going to be okay. What's the big deal?" She was the only one who was not crying. I tried to keep my composure so as not to make a big scene and joked with her about the time she cooked for me, Dr. Jerry Galloway, and Andy Braswell. She was fifteen years old then. She laughed, telling me she remembered Dr. Galloway putting money in her teddy bear for giving up her bed and cooking. There were two other sisters, Jennifer and Marciel, who helped her.

What a great time we had sitting there, remembering the past, and as we later prayed for her recovery to be rapid.

Over the next few weeks, I worked with others to find a solution. Things did not look good. The tumor was large and was located in the left front part of her head. The Doctor explained that in his opinion the tumor could be removed, but no one was talking about when that could happen. There was a young doctor with us from Detroit, Michigan who worked in a hospital there. He said, "Send the MRI on the Internet to me and let me show it to some people to see if we get a hit." A neurosurgeon happened to be walking down the hall as the MRI was coming in over the Internet. This doctor asked him if he would look at the MRI and give his opinion. He did look at it and said, "I can operate on her" after hearing of her situation. Looking at the image of the tumor, it looked as though he could just open her head and pluck it out. God answered our prayers, sending this fine doctor to help Daryelis. We were all ecstatic. I never thought we would get someone that fast, but first, Daryelis's had to have her baby. It was decided they would take the baby at seven months by C-section. The baby was named Milagro (Miracle) and put in the neonatal unit in the children's hospital. She was doing find but needed to stay in the hospital for almost two months before grandparents Chama and Derfilia, Daryelis's parents, took her home.

Working with the embassy and a missionary who lived in Panama, all the logistics were taken cared of. We obtained the necessary visa for her and her mother to travel to Detroit, Michigan, where her surgery would be performed.

The day we had long awaited arrived, the day when she would finally travel to the United States. Everyone was nervous, and there was a lot of crying on behalf of her family for no one knew what might happen. Being such a spiritual family, at the hotel that night, they all got together and prayed that Daryelis would make it to through the surgery and would return home. It was an extraordinary emotional time for they had never been separated. They were simple people leading simple lives, and everything over the next few weeks was going to be traumatic, especially the day of surgery.

My niece Jackie Marts, a registered nurse, traveled to Panama with me to bring her to the United States and to take care of all the medical needs along the way. Taking her from the hospital to our hotel, which was located close to the airport, Jackie installed the necessary IV ports so she could receive her medication on the airplane. The next morning, we all arrived early at the airport along with a lot of members of her family to say good-bye. Even though it was five o'clock in the morning, they were all there for they did not know if they would ever see her again this side of heaven. After the emotional good-byes, we proceeded through the ticket line and on through immigrations and security. Jackie was concerned that she was not capable of performing certain procedures if they became necessary. The only thing I could say was, "God will provide."

We were sitting at the gate, waiting to board the plane, when I noticed that a gentleman sitting in a wheelchair kept looking at me. I finally went over to him and said, "I am sure I know you but cannot place you." We talked a little about where we might have known each other. He said, "I know that white-headed man." We finally remembered each other for he was the director of the hospital in Santiago when we had worked on a medical team some years earlier. God did provide, and after we told him what was going on, he said he would help with whatever was needed. God always provides those necessary links that are missing. Delta Air Lines worked with us, putting her in a front seat with her mother.

The trip was uneventful, and everyone worked to help us get Daryelis through American immigrations and customs. Immigration officials were compassionate and kind, having learned through her passport why she was in the United States.

After we took off from Atlanta, it was time to administer her next dose of medicine for seizures. I could tell she really dreaded this because it was so painful. It was so painful she began to cry after Jackie began to administer the drug. I looked at Jackie and said, "We are almost there. Let's stop giving this medicine and let the doctors decide what to do next. It turned out that was a good decision because as soon as the doctor examined her, he took her off this medication and put her on one that was to be taken by mouth. We arrived in Detroit on a very cold winter night. They had never felt cold air before. Everything was beautiful and covered with snow, which brought a twinkle to their eyes for they were seeing what no Panamanian had ever seen unless they had traveled to the United States. There were people waiting with heavy coats and blankets with everybody doing their part to make them comfortable and welcome.

Daryelis was scheduled to see the surgeon, who decided to operate as soon as possible, the following day. Jackie and I returned to Alabama after getting her and her mom settled. It came time for her surgery, so I flew to Michigan to be with Derfilia, who was very afraid. She had already lost one daughter and was afraid to lose another. The morning for the surgery approached. We all gathered around the bed one final time to pray and give encouragement to her. The nurses had already shaved her head to prepare her for surgery. She was so afraid. After she returned to Panama, I found out it was not dying she was afraid of but the surgery. She was taken down the hallway and through the doors into the operating room. Derfilia started crying and was comforted by ladies from the Royal Oak Church of Christ. We had been told it would be a four-hour surgery, but four hours came and went, then five, six, and it stretched into seven. Then the doctors and the translator came into the waiting area, and they were not smiling. Our hearts stopped. The doctor began by saying that the tumor was too deep into the brain to remove. It was in the part of the brain that controls one's motor skills, like walking and using your arms. He went on to explain that if he had removed the entire tumor, she would have been paralyzed from the neck down the rest of her life. He explained that he got enough for a biopsy, and given the kind of tumor, she could more than likely live for ten to fifteen years, maybe longer. He just could not say. He tried. He gave it all he had; now it was up to God and Daryelis.

I, along with her mother, went back to ICU to see her. She looked so beautiful with her head all wrapped up in the bandage and sleeping so peacefully. We stood beside the bed, and her mother began to cry silently as she watched her beautiful daughter. I put my arm around her to comfort her while we waited for her to wake up. Her eyelids begin to flutter as she looks up and smiles at us. I tried not to shed tears. I tried to be brave and give support to her mom. It was difficult not knowing what the future would hold for Daryelis. As she became completely awake and was aware of everything happening, she started to reach up and put her arm around her mother, but she noticed her left arm would not move, and neither could she move her left leg. She begins to cry, saying, "I'm paralyzed. I have no feeling in my arm or my leg." Having already talked to her doctors, we knew she was going to have some paralysis; however, no one knew how long it would be. The doctors thought she might get the feeling back but did not know completely and were just hopeful, like everybody else. She remained in intensive care for three days. Because everything was paid for by donations, from the doctor to the anesthesiologist to the hospital, they wanted her to be moved from intensive care to another part of the hospital. The doctors had gone home for the weekend, and the nurses had fallen in love with her. They decided that if no one else needed the bed, they were going to keep her there so they could watch over her. When they finally take her out of intensive care the following Monday, the nurses began to cry as they hugged her and said good-bye. They continued coming by and visiting with her every day. Daryelis had this kind of effect on everyone who encountered her. It was heartwarming as we watched the way she smiled and her humility as she tried to calm those around her. She taught us all so much about living and about dying.

She began rehabilitation to help her learn how to walk. The nurses in this part of the hospital said, "We have brought her this far. We are not going to drop her now." Two weeks after surgery, she departed the hospital for the trip to Alabama, where she would continue her recovery before returning home to Panama.

During that time, I learned so much about helping someone who had different kinds of afflictions. I helped by picking her up, putting her in the wheelchair, and then maneuvering the wheelchair. I wanted her to see some of the sights and sounds of the United States. We drove her around Alabama, from the state capital building to the malls. There was the trip to the zoo; she saw an elephant for the first time and took her first train ride. Everywhere she went, she had a bandanna tied about her head, which added, I thought, to her beauty. She never complained and kept apologizing for being a burden, which I assured her she was not. We took her to Maxwell Air Force Base, and with the help of one of the crew chiefs of a C-130 airplane, we picked her up, placed her in the pilot seat, and gave her an experience many only dream of. She laughed as she posed for pictures with the airmen who worked on the plane.

There was a big party in her honor at my house with many people dropping by to say good-bye. What a wonderful time she was having, but after a two-week stay, it was time for her to return to Panama. Our flight arrived in Panama City late at night with all of her family waiting at the airport with local television stations recording the return of the mother who had never seen her child. Her father was standing there with a big bouquet of flowers. This was his first trip to an airport. It was emotional as we watched her sister place the child in her arms as she was wheeled out of the customs area into the waiting area. Many people were there to welcome her home; she was now surrounded by so many who loved her. Many tears were shed as they watched her look at her baby.

The following day, we drove the 150 miles back to the Sanson community where she lived, arriving there around nine at night. There were about fifty people waiting at the house for her arrival. They begin to cook chicken soup and rice this late at night for it was a time of celebration, and no one was talking about going to bed.

As time went on, Daryelis tried to adapt to being back home and tried to walk without help. We all tried to make it comfortable for her, but it was still hard. We built her a cement sidewalk from the house to the outdoor toilet and made her a handrail out of bamboo so she could maneuver when she needed to go to the bathroom. We wanted her to be able to have more independence for she felt so useless trying to learn how to get around. It came time for me to return to the United States. Daryelis had become so dependent on me for she was like my very own daughter, but I had responsibilities with my own family and knew I must go. She needed to try to make a life for her and her daughter Miracle with whatever time God was going to give her.

I returned to Panama in early June with a group from Florida to look at an area where we might be able to work. I stayed in the home of Daryelis, enjoying the hospitality. One night, Daryelis began to vomit and have severe headaches. Around two in the morning, her father asked me about taking her to the doctor in

Panama City. I told him we would leave as soon as we could in the morning. The problem was it rained, and the road was almost impassable; therefore, we had to get someone who had a four-wheel drive to drive us to where I had my car parked, about fifteen miles away. We arrived in Panama City having already made arrangements to go to a private hospital. We had also made arrangements for her to see a neurologist as soon as we arrived. The prognosis was not good. The tumor had begun to bleed, and pressure was building up in her brain. She was put on medication to lower the pressure. The doctor informed us that he believed she might live for a period of weeks and not months. If an operation was performed, he believed she might live a year but did not know what kind of year it would be. This was shocking news to everyone

    I decided to go very early to the hospital, finding her father by her bed. I told him to go and get something to eat and I would sit with Daryelis for a while. While he was gone, I sat down on the bed and talked to Daryelis. I said, "Daryelis, everybody has been saying what they would like to have happen, but what do you want?" What she said shocked me but really was no surprise knowing of her faith in God and the faith of her family. She said, "No more operations!" I replied, "Daryelis, you know if you do not have an operation, you cannot live very long." She looked at me and smiled, and said, "Everything is going to be okay." To be honest, I was at loss for words, so I hugged her and told her how much I loved her and how much she meant to so many people and to this ministry. I told her that her faith was an example to all of us. She had reached a peace that comes only through a close relationship with God and knowing that heaven is just around the corner.

    We made arrangements for her to stay with her uncle close to the city where she would have medical help when she needed it. We installed an air conditioner in her room so she would be more comfortable.

It came time for me to depart for I had to return home to the United States. I had stayed as long as I possibly could. I would like to have stayed longer for I developed such a close relationship with this family, and she was like one of my own children, but I had other responsibilities. I decided not to go back for a final visit due to the emotional ties it would have on her and me.

My airplane had no sooner landed in Atlanta when my cell phone rang. It was Daryelis. She said, "Where are you?" I said I was in Atlanta on my way home, and she began to cry. I did not know what to say for she felt if I could just be there, everything would be okay. I told her I loved her for she had become such a great part of our lives and if I did not see her again, I would see her in heaven. The following day, I received another phone call, this time from her sister Marciel, who was frantic. "She will not wake up. She will not wake up." Having dealt with this many times as a minister, I knew the end was near for she was now in a coma. A short time later, I received a call that Daryelis had died. Our ministry paid for the expenses for the funeral for the family had no money. Hundreds of people attended her funeral for her family was so loved by so many. Daryelis had made her impact upon the lives of us all. We had given it all we had; however, in the end, God had other plans for her.

A DISTORTED PICTURE

When I first met a young lady by the name of Anayansi Sanchez, I was moved deeply because I could see she had an affliction that she was ashamed of. It distorted her appearance, taking away from her beauty. I had seen her come to the church building many times but never really got to know her. She was thirteen years old, living with her mother and four sisters along with her stepfather. She was attractive but very shy, never saying one word to anyone. She had little self-confidence but seemed to be a very sweet child. Being an outgoing person, I wanted to get to know her better, so I went up and introduced myself. She already knew who I was because I had been there so many times. They live in the community of Torti and attended the Torti Church of Christ. They were a family with many struggles. There were five beautiful girls and all needing special things and never enough money. A family from Kentucky became involved in helping them, but Anayansi needed special attention. In my investigation, I found she was very smart in school but had struggles because of this affliction she had had since she was three years old.

I had noticed her left eye for she always kept it closed or tried to hide it because she was conscious of people looking at her. The eyeball itself was white and was very difficult for her to cover up. One day, her mother came to me, asking if perhaps on the next medical team, a doctor could examine her. We had a team coming to Meteti, so I planned for her to be there on the first day, which was Sunday. She had been examined in Panama City many years earlier. Due to a small eye irritation that turned into an infection that went untreated, this caused her to lose sight in this eye. I made arrangements for them to travel to Metetí and be the first to see the ophthalmologist.

As I approached the clinic, I noticed Anayansi and her mother standing outside, and both were crying. Being the nosy person that I am, I asked them what the problem was. Her mother told me that the doctors said nothing could be done for her eye for the retina and surrounding tissue had been destroyed by the infection. However, the globe itself was intact. I hugged them both and promised we would do everything in our power to make her look like a normal person. I did not have a clue how I was going to bring this one about.

Years before, I had bound upon myself a rule—never promise someone something I could not deliver. The question I asked myself was, why did I do this on this day? Why did I tell this thirteen-year-old we would have her looking beautiful like everybody else? I saw them off on the bus for their return trip to Torti. Over the next several days, I agonized over the promise I had made, wondering what I had done and if I would be able to help Anayansi.

The first thing I did was send her to an ophthalmologist in Panama City to see how we could relieve her pain for she was in constant pain with this eye. "Why is she in so much pain?" I asked but received no answer. It was suggested that they might even have to remove the eye and install an artificial one. I did not buy that even though I am not a doctor; I just could not see them removing her eye. The doctor in Panama City cleaned out the eye to help relieve some of the pain. I told her I was going to make some phone calls when I return to the United States to see what could be done for I had made a promise and I wanted to keep it. Upon returning from Panama, I immediately talked with my brother-in-law, Jack Cates, an optician from Montgomery, Alabama, and his father, Coleman, about what her possibilities were. They in turn contacted an ophthalmologist they knew and inquired of him the best course of action. He said he could not make a determination without first seeing her and was willing to see her at no cost if she was to come to the United States. With a letter from the ophthalmologist in Montgomery and from Cates Optical, we applied for her and her mother a visa, which was issued. We raised the money for travel expenses. They arrived in Montgomery excited for this was the first time either mother or daughter had traveled outside of Panama. This was the first time they had flown on a plane, had a ride on a train, as well as many other firsts. Just having them come to the United States was an exciting time for everyone.

The next stop was the office of a Montgomery ophthalmologist. We were ushered in and treated just as we were paying a lot of money. The doctor was an extraordinary man with a wonderful heart. With a young man by the name of Chris Taylor translating, the doctor began his examination. It was not long until he had an answer. He said, "The globe itself is like a burr with stickers all over. Every time she blinked, it was like her eyelid was coming down over the stickers, causing intense pain." Can you imagine if every time you blink your eye, you would have excruciating pain that would lead to infection and then to so many other problems? The question was, how are we going to remedy this problem? The doctor said removing the eyeball was not an option for there would be far more complications. He suggested a contact lens that looks like the other eye—a prosthetic lens. He wrote out two different prescriptions to be taken back to Cates Optical. One was for a prosthesis lens and the other for a medicine she would need to put in her eye for the rest of her life to keep down the infection.

We returned to Cates Optical, where Jack Cates did all the measurements for the new prosthetic lens. After about two weeks, her new lens came in, and it was time for her appointment with Cates Optical to install the lens. Of course, the lens was a contact that was made to look like her other eye. Jack began to show her how to put the lens in and told her she could not return to Panama until she was able to install it and remove it. There were many tears over the next couple of weeks while she was learning how to install, take out, and care for her new lens. The lens was such a perfect match that it changed the entire look of her face. Jack said, "When she looked in the mirror, her smile said it all for it covered her entire face, and even the sadness that seemed to embellish her beautiful face went away. There is a twinkle in her eye that was not there when she first entered our office." We all shed tears when we saw the difference it made in her. It gave her a new lease on life, great confidence, and it increased her beauty a hundredfold. She now can hold her head high and look at others without people staring. The change that came about her was so noticeable that people even wondered if this was the same person. She became involved more in school activities, in her community, and more especially, in her church, where she became a leader among the young people. Although still very shy for that is her nature, she has a self-confidence that she did not have before. What if we had just written her off and said "Nothing can be done" or "I'm sorry, we cannot help you?" Where would she be? What would have been her future? I try to instill in others that even in the most difficult cases, one has to try for not to try is to be defeated, and I will not accept defeat unless I have put forth my best effort.

This advice is for every avenue of life, and we need to encourage our young people to never give up just because life is not what we thought it ought to be. Too many times we have seen people give up, and when they give up, life ceases to exist even though they may go on living.

We should all know that sometimes it takes each one of us as Christians to step outside our own comfort zones. Yes, it takes us walking by faith and not by sight. We stepped out in faith, knowing there was someone somewhere out there who could bring change to this young person's life. It did take a lot of people and a good bit of money to make it all happen, but in the end, the results were tremendous, even greater than our expectation. God is good and provides the blessings people need in the lowest time of their life, but he often works through people like you and me. In the favorite expression of Demar Elam, missionary to the Philippines, "God is good. God is good all the time."

Anayansi is now married to a fine man and has just had her first child. She is very involved in her church and her family.

Each one of us must never write anyone off before we have put forth every effort, exhausted every means, and prayed diligently for a good outcome. And never forget, it is God who delivers. We are his instruments, and he desires to use us in the completion and fulfilling of his will.

These are the words of Anayansi:

> One of the greatest lessons in my lifetime is the day Panama Missions came into my life. I first of all thank God for all that was done for me during very difficult times. I am grateful to Larry and Betsy Brady and their family for they are such wonderful people. I am so happy God allowed me to meet them for I have adopted them as my family. They have helped people all over Panama just like they helped me, and I am so grateful for this blessing in my life. I had no hope of ever finding a solution to my problem until one day, God sent this mission to help me. They are people with such big hearts, and they do not care who we are or where we are from, but they love us and help us. Because of what they did for me, I am now a different person.
>
> The most important thing about this program is their goal to teach people about God's love even though we

do not have the financial means to do anything. I know God is always with us through the bad and the good. I am thankful to all the people that work with Panama Missions because through their efforts many will be helped.

Anayansi Sanchez, Torti, Panama

GOD IS BIG

They were lined up to see audiologist Ken Pollard from Macon, Georgia. This was our first time having an audiologist accompany us on a medical mission. When he first asked about going, I told him that we have never done this, and I did not know if he would even have any patience. Discussing this with the local medical people, they did not believe very many people would come to see the audiologist because most were not familiar with this. How wrong we all were for little did we know how busy this retired audiologist would be. He was accompanied by Gates Winters, who attended the same church in Georgia that he did. Gates was a retired baseball coach and was traveling on his first mission to assist his friend Ken Pollard. They would make a tremendous team, working together for Gates, entertaining people with the noises he made and with his funny gestures. He was a natural working with people who did not understand his language.

There was no place for the audiologist to work in the small clinic, so we put him in a small room where he had to run his wires out the window to the generator. The clinic was in a community west of Torti named Plattinillia. This was a beautiful community nestled back in the mountains.

The people lined up to see the audiologist. He was the last one through every day. He took people into a small room and closed the door to give them a hearing examination. I watched the people put on the earmuffs and raise their hand if they heard the sound and lower their hand if they did not. Ken had worked out a system that proved you don't always have to have a translator for some things just naturally translate themselves. It was fascinating to watch the people respond to him. Most of the people who came in to the clinic that could not hear very well had ears impacted with earwax. Sometimes Ken could remove it easily, and other times, it took quite a while as he had to put in a medicine to dissolve the earwax. Their hearing was restored after he cleaned their ears. It was amazing to watch the transformation of their faces when all he did was remove the earwax.

After Ken had examined the hearing of an elderly lady, she replied, "I went to Panama City, and they told me, 'You are old, and old people lose their hearing.'" Ken joked with her and made her feel comfortable, and then he installed a solar-powered hearing aid. She could hear crystal clear out of an ear that before was deaf.

People saw what was happening with this lady as she began to cry, and her daughter began crying, and everyone knew God's power had been demonstrated here today. It was a miracle for them. Truly a miracle! The little lady said over and over again, God is big. This is all new to them, not knowing that her hearing could be made better by such a simple instrument, something so small yet performing such a great task.

Modern technology came into the mountains of Panama and brought with it the joy of hearing.

However, Ken Pollard's work was not done for there were many others who lined up, hoping to be the recipients of one of those miraculous instruments. A teenage girl was standing in line, waiting patiently for her turn. Normally, you would not see someone this young standing in this line, waiting to have her hearing checked. She waited a good part of the day for her time, and when her time came, Ken found she had an extreme hearing loss, one so bad it affected her in school and in every area of her life. She talked loudly because she was unable to hear herself speaking. She has had this hearing loss all of her life, and nothing had been done to correct it. Further evaluation found her hearing loss could be corrected with a hearing aid. The problem was Ken would have to return to the United States, have the device made, and return it to Panama. After much conversation, he assured her she would have a hearing aid in a few short months. He lived up to his promise for when he returned to the United States, he had her hearing aid made. He also had a backup made so she would always have one.

The next time I returned to Panama, I had in my possession this young lady's hearing aid. One thing we failed to get was her name. How did we overlook her name? But with an inquiry, she was easily located because people know one another in these areas. I made arrangements for her to meet me at a local restaurant in the community of Torti with her mother. She was a beautiful young lady, and I noticed she wasn't smiling when I initially met with her to give her her hearing aid. I took it out of the box and placed it in her ear, and immediately, a big smile came upon her face. As the sun rose in the morning, her smile radiated all around us. I only wished Ken could have been there to see the results of his work. It was all I could do to contain my emotions when I saw her reaction. This small instrument would change this child's life. She would have a new lease on life. Not only would she have a new lease on life but all of us standing there were touched by her reaction. It also brought about a change in all of us.

However, this young lady is only part of the story of bringing an audiologist to Panama. Ken Pollard knew his work was not finished and returned over and over again because he was touched and so moved by what he could do with the training he had received given his God-given talents. Not only did he use his talents, he used it with such love, compassion, and kindness, always smiling, always encouraging everyone that stood before him. He took his time to take care of the needs of the people for some of them required a lot of time due to their individual situation.

Such was an older gentleman who came into the clinic. As we would say, he could not hear it thunder. He had a big smile upon his face, but he was in a lot of discomfort. When his turn came, he sat there for his examination and, in doing so, experienced more discomfort while Ken dug around in his ear, trying to find out what his problem was. It did not take long for Ken to determine the cause of his hearing loss and the cause of the pain he was experiencing. There seemed to be something lodged in each ear. He could not just reach in and pull it out for it was lodged against the eardrum. He brought with him an instrument he used that looked like a large metal syringe to remove foreign objects from their ears. It held several ounces of water, and when he would put it up to the ear, a plastic bag was also held in place by a helper. Ken would take and force the water into the ear canal, hoping that the object would dislodge itself. However, with this man, the object had been in there quite some time, and earwax had developed around it, making it difficult to remove. Over and over he flushed the ear, hoping the object would come out. After almost an hour of working on the one ear, the object popped out into the bag. No one could believe what they were witnessing. A large cockroach evidently had crawled into his ear canal while he was asleep and died, not being able to get back out. The man began smiling and for obvious reasons. He was able to hear, and the roaring in his head immediately got better. People began to gather around to look, not believing what they were seeing. Ken immediately began flushing the opposite ear for now he probably knew what was in the man's ear. Could it be that he would have another cockroach in the other ear? That is actually what was there and was harder to get out than the first one, but after over an hour and a lot of water, out pops another cockroach to the amazement of everyone. I do not suppose I have ever seen such a big smile or a sense of relief from anyone as I did from this good man.

Ken had to take a break for not only was he hot and tired, but he just needed time to relax and enjoy the moment and to think about what he had accomplished, what God had done through his hands and the relief this man had to be feeling at this moment. I do not have the words to express the greatness of medical missions and what people accomplish in them. This man had been suffering for months with pain in his ears, and he had nowhere to go.

The year before, we had been working out of the Clinic of Hope located in the Darién Province. Many people came and went during the week with all types of medical conditions. Hearing evaluations were being given, and there was no end to the line. Most of them had minor hearing problems that were corrected by removing the earwax. Some were evaluated for major hearing loss, and others received a hearing aid. There were just not enough resources, and people had to be selected for the seriousness of their situation. It always weighed heavily upon our hearts when we could not help every single individual, but as the woman with the alabaster box, we did what we could with what we had. This was no exception with Ken Pollard. He did what he could.

There was one man who had never learned how to talk who came into the clinic with his mother. He was forty-two years old and had never been to the doctor with his speech and hearing problems. He was born with it, and consequently, he had lived with it all of his life. When it was announced on the radio program *The Voice of the Frontier* that hearing evaluations would be given at the Clinic of Hope, his mother decided they would make the trip just to see if there was a possibility something could be done for his hearing and speech. When Ken checked his hearing, he found it was correctable, and having one of the solar-powered hearing aids, he put it in to see what would happen. What happened next was nothing short of a miracle because this forty-two-year-old man who had never heard a sound in his life now was able to hear very clearly. So often people born with abnormalities in third world countries just live with them because they know there's nothing that can be done or they do not have the money to pursue a cure. The man had never learned how to talk, and now, at forty-two years old, he will need to learn how to communicate. Is it not amazing what God can do through the hands of others? We have all heard it said, "God has no hands but my hands. He has no feet but my feet, no voice but my voice to do his blessed work." Ken Pollard made the same statement many other medical people have made over the years, "God has given me a talent, and I want to use it to benefit others." This man received his hearing through the use of modern technology, but if you were to ask this family how he received his hearing, they would say it's a miracle.

During a mission trip in Torti, Panama, it was decided we would take the audiologist to a school of Santa Rosa located several miles to the west. This is a school that Panama Missions had adopted. We built a kindergarten and donated funds for the parents to build a kitchen. Ken took with him his instruments and set up a small examination station in the middle of the school. The classes lined up for the examination of each child. After the first two or three students, Ken knew he had his work cut out for him for every student had a loss of hearing due to a buildup of earwax, and most of it impacted because of the parents taking Q-tips or something like a Q-tip to clean the ear, and in doing so, they would pack the wax around the eardrum. Some even had ear infections due to people digging in their ears, which can damage the eardrum. Some of the earwax could not be removed, and ear drops to soften the wax were put in with cotton. The children were told to come to Torti the following day to be seen. As Ken was working, he looked up at me and said, "After this is over, we are going to get all the parents of the community and have them bring their Q-tips, and we are going to have a marshmallow roasting while we burn all these things." He laughs and says, "This is the worst thing people can do to their children's ears when they think they are helping them." The teachers were amazed after every child's ears were clean and how they could hear so much better. They knew it was going to improve their schoolwork. Something as simple as ear cleaning brought so much gratification to the one serving. Using what God had given, him he shares with others.

Ken Pollard writes the following:

> One day in Torti, at the opening of their health center for the Panama Missions's medical team, Larry introduced the Indian chief's family to Gates Winters and me in our small audiology test room. The native beauty of this family, especially the youngest preschool daughter, was remarkable as was the kindness shown to us. There were multitalented people from all over the United States using their God given skills to help others. Then there were the Peace Corps volunteers who served as our interpreters throughout the week. However, the giant hook that gets you is the gracious and sweet people that live in the Darien province. I remember the smiles elicited when a teenage girl as well as the older people heard through a solar-powered hearing aid. My reward was a native root given to me after one mothers forty-two-year-old son was successfully fitted in Sanson with a hearing aid. Who can forget the old man of Sanson happily waving good-bye as we drove by on the last day. He arrived with one deaf ear, and I prayed that the other would be cerumen filled. Two days of cerumen softening and ear irrigation were required to restore sound to this man's life, as it was for many.
>
> Back at home in Macon, Georgia, I saw three generations of women train teenage girls to sew dresses for Operation Christmas Joy culminating in over five hundred

dresses for Darién's children. Throughout the year Coach Gates Winters continue to collect baseball equipment for the children of the Darien province so they could play little league baseball. Because of his efforts several communities now have baseball teams with one team representing the Darien province in Panama in the playoffs. All of this because a retired coach found a mission that changed his life even though he is unable to return to Panama. While cleaning a homesite for concrete flooring, Gates paid the price of breathing an unhealthy host in his lungs that almost killed him. Even though his physician grounded him, Gates still yearns to return to the Panama.

                Ken Pollard, audiologist, Macon, Georgia

THE MAN WITH A BIG SMILE

There have been many people I have met that have touched my heart and have had an impact in my life during the past twenty-eight years. Over the years I have met people with their smiles, humility, their patience and their ability to get along with anybody and everybody and truly love being part of a mission group. Such a man was Victor Newell, who lived in Colón with his wife. I was asked by the local preacher Avaroe Earlington to go with him to visit Victor and his wife for the purpose of studying the Bible. Victor was not a Christian, and his wife was. We walked down an alley to the small apartment, which consisted of one room with no bathroom, not even an outdoor toilet or shower. They had to use a community toilet and shower. When I knocked on the door, a fairly large black man opened the door with a big smile on his face. I immediately took a liking to Victor, as would anyone who ever met him. Everyone fell in love with him, always requesting him to be part of their team as a translator. He spoke fluent English as did his wife for the family was originally from Jamaica; however, Victor had lived in Panama all of his life.

I asked him if it was possible for me to study the Bible with him. A good friend and preacher from Luverne, Alabama, J. W. Furr, was with me, and like me, he liked Victor from the very first meeting. Victor agreed for the Bible study, perhaps so he would not be disrespectful. Whatever his purpose, he did not know nor did any of us realize just how this entire ministry was about to be changed and what plans God had for him. How can one individual change a ministry? I did not think it was possible until I met Victor, who was not a Christian, did not want to be a Christian, and to his own admittance, said he was serving the devil. I do not believe Victor was being mean or even trying to be disrespectful, but rather, he was being honest about the direction of his life. We open the Bible and begin to talk about the love of God and how God could take away the sins of the world through his son, Jesus Christ. Victor had some questions along the way about the life he had lived and the ability of God to take away his sins. We studied for almost two hours with Victor, listening very attentively, and every now and then, as I have said, he asked questions, but mostly, he listened. I got to the place in the study where I felt I needed to ask Victor if he would make a commitment to Jesus Christ and obey his Lord in baptism. When I asked him this question, Victor just sat there for he was always very slow to speak and careful of what he said. I learned that he never wanted to offend anyone. Even in this study, he was careful because all of this was new to him. He was very sincere in everything he said and everything he did. He loved his wife deeply and was committed to her, yet he had never followed her in the religious path she had taken. Victor looked at me, and then he looked at the others, and finally, he looked at his wife and said, "Fifty-two years I have served the devil, and that has not worked. It is time to do something else. I want to be a Christian today." I sat there for a moment before I spoke. I said, "Victor, you will never regret this decision. No one regrets doing what God wants them to do.

We traveled across town to the closest place we could baptize him, and the local preacher, Alvaroe Earlington, baptized Victor into Christ. I can truly say that Victor never looked back; he never regretted his decision for he truly was a changed man from that day.

It was not long until Alvaroe, who also was fluent in English, decided to travel to United States and work with the Spanish-speaking church in North Alabama, leaving me without a translator. I called Victor, asking him if he could come with me and translate on a mission trip. He informed me that this would be new to him and there was so much he did not know but that he wanted to learn. He agreed to go with me into the Darién Province, a place he had never been. He had heard about it, and what he had heard was not good, and he was nervous about traveling into this part of Panama. Only 10 percent of the population of Panama ever venture into the Darién Province for all considered it to be dangerous. Victor said, "God will be with us, so I don't have to worry, so I will go with you." From that day forward, every time I came to Panama, Victor would be waiting for me either at the airport or at the hotel where he knew I would be staying. Others began to use Victor in their mission groups. Each one came under his charm. He became a voice telling the wonderful story of Jesus over and over. He became the voice for doctors, dentists, and nurses. One doctor joked that Victor knew almost what to tell the patient to do and how to take the medicine before he even said anything because he learned so much.

One day, we were in Santa Fe, Darién, with a medical team when a young lady who had traveled seven hours by boat and one and a half by bus to get to our clinic arrived. She was very ill, suffering from a lot of pain in her stomach. She was referred to Panama City, where she was put in the hospital, finding out she had a tumor that needed to be removed. I visited her with Victor in the hospital. While there, I asked her where she lived. She replied she lived the community Unión Chocó, seven hours by boat from the end of the road, which ended in the town of Yavisa. I decided that on my next mission trip, I would go and visit her if I could obtain permission and get security from the police for this town was located close to the Colombian border. Asking Victor to go, he stumbled around, trying to come up with an excuse why he should not go before he answered, but finally said, "I will go with you, and God will protect us." He was visibly afraid. He informed me he was going places with me he never dreamed he would go in his own country. We did make the trip, and the first person we saw as we were pulling up to the bank was Nora as she was washing her clothes in the River. We had a wonderful visit. Victor was at my side every moment. My police escort were just behind me, following me everywhere I went, so Victor stuck with me like glue. I kidded with him and said there was a rebel behind every tree. He gave me that big laugh that he always gives everybody, saying, "I'm with you, brother."

During the building of the Clinic of Hope, Victor was there to translate for any worker that needed help with a translation. He was the only translator and was running everywhere, translating. People would holler "Victor," and Victor would come running. "Victor," someone else would call, and Victor would come running. This went on all day every day. Two men who fell in love with Victor on this trip were Allen Gunn and Bill Watts. Victor really had an impact upon them because of his patience, his love for others, his kindness, and his willing to always be there, doing anything requested of him. There happened to be a parakeet in the tree that was there every day. One day, before the end of the trip, someone heard "Victor, Victor, Victor." It was the parakeet who had picked up on the name of Victor because everybody called his name so much.

Our medical team was working in the town of Meteti, Darien where Victor was serving as the translator for the dentist.

Victor has had most of his teeth pulled; however, there was one right in the front that was left and was loose. The dentist and his wife had great compassion for him, knowing he was having some problems with that tooth. They asked him if he would like it pulled, and he gladly accepted the offer. He would not ask them to pull it because he never complained. He never asked for anything for himself. I suppose this is one of the great traits he had, and he influenced everyone around him. They did pull the tooth, which now left him completely toothless and in need of dentures. One of the doctors paid for Victor to get him a new set of dentures. He never learned to eat with them, so he always pulled them out and put them in his pocket when it came time to eat. No one ever commented to Victor about this, thinking we might offend him; however, I found an occasion to question him about it. I thought perhaps something was wrong with the dentures and we could help them get them repaired. He simply said to me, "No, brother, everything is fine. They're just a little loose." I let him know that they could be adjusted, but he pretty much was satisfied with wearing those dentures and just put them in his pocket when he ate.

We all noticed Victor slowing down for it did not seem he had the same energy he had always possessed nor the enthusiasm; however, he still never complained. He only asked if it was possible that I could help him get some of those Tylenol tablets that help him sleep at night. He said for some reason he was having a lot of pain but had not been to the doctor. He planned on going and said so, but to my knowledge, he never went.

In 2009, Panama Missions traveled to the town of Yavisa with a surgical team from Denver, Colorado, and other medical professionals from around the country. Of course, Victor was there, translating this time for two doctors, Dr. Duke Jennings and Doctor Stan Combs. Doctor Combs was extremely taken by Victor and his loving attitude toward everyone. Doctor Jennings told me Victor was not his old self. He seemed sick and tired and could not breathe well nor could he stay awake. After two days, Dr. Jennings and Doctor Combs decided they needed to examine Victor to find out why he was so sick. Doctor Stan Combs from Los Angeles California was the first to notice something wasn't right with Victor and proceeded to do an examination. It was at this time they knew Victor was extremely ill even suggesting it might be cancer.

He was taking pain medication they were giving him, but it did not seem to help in relieving his pain. They listened to his breathing and found there was no activity in his left lung, meaning there was no air in his lung. They tried to get him to return to Colón so he could be checked out at a local hospital in his hometown. He refused, saying he wanted to complete the mission. The following day, I insisted he return. We sent him back on our vehicle to Panama City, where he caught a bus home. Dr. Jennings gave him the money to go directly to the hospital for a chest X-ray to find out what the problem was. After we returned to Panama City, we discovered that Victor was in the hospital, and the diagnosis was not good. They thought he might have cancer. I called Victor and talked to him on the telephone. His prognosis was not good. Dr. Jennings called and talked to his doctor. He suggested if it was money that was keeping him from getting good care there were those in the United States who would pay. The doctor assured him that everything that could be done was being done. Calls were coming in, saying, "Whatever Victor needs, we will make sure he gets the best care money can buy." Again, the doctor assured Dr. Jennings that Victor was getting good care and would receive everything he needed. I talked to Victor just before I left Panama, saying, "Victor, I love you. Everybody loves you, and if I don't see you again, I'll see you in heaven." Victor said to me, "I'll be all right. I'll be all right." His doctor related to Dr. Jennings, "If this man does not make it to heaven, then there is no need in me trying. I do not know what religion he is, but when I come into the room, he would not let me take care of him until I have taken care of everybody else. He is always smiling." What a wonderful commentary on the life of one of the greatest men I've ever met in Panama. During the course of this ministry, I have met many people, including the president of Panama, the first lady, ambassadors, and other influential people, but never one like Victor. Victor had no money, no car, no luxury; however, Victor has something money could not buy—assurance of a heavenly crown promised to him by the God of heaven.

Less than a month after Victor Newell was told he had cancer, he went on to meet the Lord and took his place at the right hand of God. Money flooded in to pay for all the expenses of Victor's funeral. His wife was afflicted with Alzheimer's disease and needed special care, which Victor had always so lovingly done. Again, money flooded in to take care of her. She died a few months later. Like Victor, her funeral was paid for by Victor's many brothers and sisters in Christ throughout the United States.

Never was anyone so greatly loved by so many people as this great man. He won our hearts not by money but by his kindness, his sweet disposition, and his Christ like spirit.

When the Clinic of Hope was dedicated, it was done so in memory of Victor Newell, a faithful servant who had such a sweet spirit and served as an example to us all. His picture hangs on the wall upstairs in the living quarters so all of us can continually be reminded of how he touched our lives.

Anayansi Sanchez after her transformation.

Thelma Brady fits clothing on children thus starting the sewing for Panama Program.

Omaida Campos and Ambassador Linda Watt visit during a visit to the Darien province.

Young people from Panama visit with Gov. Bob Riley of Alabama during Panama Missions Cultural Exchange

Childen who live in poverty. We delivered gifts in
2010 during severe flooding in Panama.

In the Rain forest of Panama on the Chucunaque
River with Jose Calderon

On the Chucunaque River

Crew on 2nd floor during the construction of the Clinic of Hope

Clinic of Hope Sanson, Darien Panama

Embera Indian Village Darien, Panama

Ipeti Kuna village

With the children in El Real, Darien

Four youth from Panama visit Alabama Christian Academy during a cultural exchange visit.

Santa AKA Larry Brady and First Lady Vivian Torijos of Panama in the Hospital del Ninos

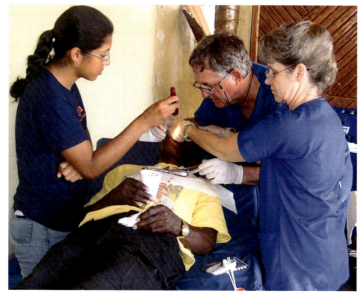

Dr Jerry Galloway and his wife Joy along with their translator, Melissa Valdes Sanchez extract a tooth.

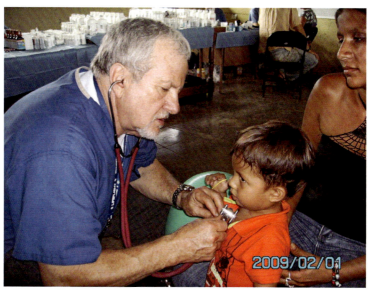

Dr. Duke Jennings medical director of Panama Missions examines A child during a medical campaign.

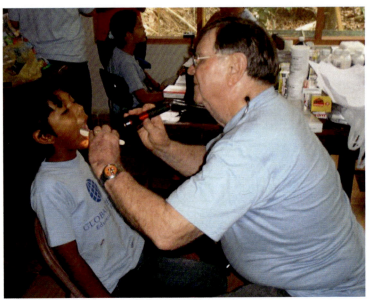
Dr Joe Wilhite Examines a child during a medical visit.

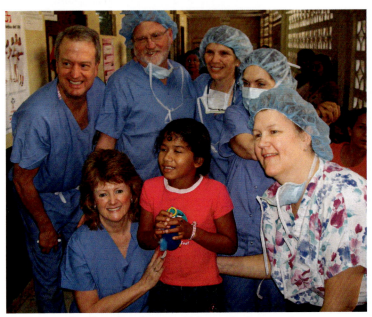
Dr. Russ Burcham and his surgical team who restored the sight of this 10 year old girl.

Betsy Brady delivers hygene bags to the mothers of children in the Hospital del Ninos

Burn Victim with Santa in Hospital del Ninos during Christmas 2009

Danely Cardenas Miranda and Larry Brady at graduation from Faulkner University

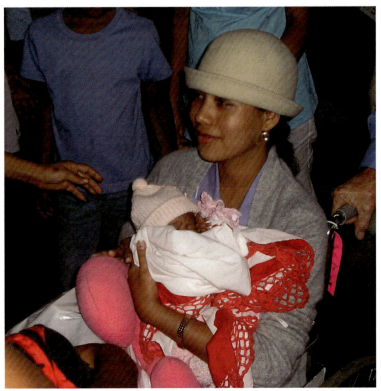

Daryelis Sanez upon arrival at Tucumen airport in Panama united with her baby. Six weeks before she under went brain surgery

Embera Children like to entertain us with their dancing.

In Memory Victor Newell

Larry Brady's granddaughter Emma and her new friend Josilina show how hard it is to leave new friends behind.

Max and Diane Edrington with a former chief of the Embera people.

Yaritza Chami demonstrating the Embera culture upon a visit to the United States.

FULFILLING A PROMISE

She lived in a village, Unión Chocó, seven hours from where our medical team was working in the town of Metetí. She said she heard over the radio that there would be a medical team from the United States, so she made plans to make the trip, hoping she might receive help for a problem that had plagued her and was getting worse. With her small child, she traveled by boat to the town of Yavisa. From there, she must take a bus for another hour. She arrived at the clinic late in the evening the day before she would see one of the Panama Mission doctors. Waiting patiently in line for her turn, she was finally directed to see a doctor everyone called Dr. Dave. Dr. Dave and his wife work together and were some of the sweetest people and were so compassionate toward those who sat across from them. The children were first given a piece of candy by Doctor Dave's wife as she played with the children. They seem to be trying to get the people to be at ease. After this initiation, they would then ask what the problem was. This young mother's name was Nora, an Embera Indian. You could generally tell who was Indian and who was not by their clothes. Embera women always wore a beautiful colored wraparound dress and sometimes would have different designs painted on their arms and faces. She was very tired after such a long trip. I could see that Dr. Dave was very concerned about her after his initial consultation and examination. I was called over to talk to them about what was next to see if we were able to help them. It seemed that Nora had a possible tumor in her neck and at least two lumps in her breasts.

One of the big problems of people who live in indigenous villages throughout the world is the lack of proper medical care. It is an incorrect statement and conclusion to say this is the way they live and they just accept it. We have found people living with horrendous diseases and dying of terrible pain, diseases we do not allow to go untreated in the United States. Even among the poorest of the poor, these things are not allowed to go untreated. Unless a medical team such as ours comes into the area, there is little they can do. Most third world countries do not have systems set up throughout wherein people can get help. In Panama, they must often travel to Panama City to see a doctor. This can be very expensive, so they just live with it. Nora was a young mother in her early twenties and had an entire life ahead of her. She loved her culture, which I personally have grown to love and respect. After questioning her to find out if she was willing to do what was necessary to follow up with doctors in Panama City, I made the arrangements for her to go see a doctor at the public hospital in Panama City. Upon our arrival and initial evaluation, she was admitted to the hospital. We were happy to hear that Nora had three benign tumors. However, they needed to be removed because they would continue to grow. One of the tumors in her neck was fairly large.

I visited her in the hospital and was able to assist them with some money for her husband had traveled from the Darién to be with her. The surgery was successful, and after a one-month stay in the hospital, Nora returned to her family. I told her before she left the hospital that I would like to visit her community sometime. Little did I know where her community was located.

On my next trip to Panama, I decided I was going to fulfill my promise to her and made arrangements with the police in Yavisa to go with me and use one of their fast boats. I purchased fifty-five gallons of fuel, and after the fuel was loaded into the boat, we set out on our adventure. As we traveled southeast toward Columbia, I was truly amazed at the beauty all along the way. God created a beautiful place when he created the Darién Province. The trip that took Nora seven hours traveling by piragua took us around three hours. When we arrived, the first person I saw was Nora in the edge of the water, washing her clothes. She was ecstatic to see us for she never believed I would ever make the trip to visit her and her family as I had promised. I hugged her and told her how excited I was to be in her community. She immediately motioned for us to follow her to her house. This was my first time traveling this deep into Darién, and I was truly amazed at the *National Geographic* moment I was experiencing. No gringos had ever visited here, so I was somewhat of a novelty as the children began to follow us around. Two children, one on each side, grabbed my hand and held on as I walked throughout the village. Nora was happy to introduce me to the local chief, and then we went to her house. They all laughed at me as I began to climb the pole that led up into the house. It was just a pole with notches cut out for your toes, and gringo toes seemed to be larger than the Indian toes. It seemed that way to me anyway. Their cook stove consisted of a box full of dirt and three small logs pushed together with the pot sitting in the middle. The logs would continue to be pushed inward as the fire burned. I sat there in the hammock provided for me for they supposed this gringo with the white hair was tired. They supposed right for not only was I tired, I was also hungry but did not let on to them because of obvious reasons. I have eaten in many of their villages, but they had nothing cooking, and I knew I would not be there long enough for them to begin cooking a meal for me, which would have consisted of making soup out of one of the chickens underneath the house. I also did not want to eat up their meager rations. I made a big deal out of not being all that hungry, and I would just eat some

Vienna sausages and crackers and chase it with my water. Of course, there were children surrounding me, so I was prepared, bringing with me candy. When you get out candy in the villages, you really get a big following not only of children but of adults. They enjoyed the treats I had brought. I shared my sausages and crackers with Nora and her family. Everyone seemed to enjoy the food so I decided to let them have it for it was not going to last anyway and we would soon be back in Sanson.

I asked Nora how her health was and if she was having any discomfort from her previous surgery. She said she was doing well and had not experienced a lot of pain. Her father continued thanking me over and over for what we had done for his daughter. I talked to some of them about how Jesus had given us an example by helping those who need it the most, that it was our responsibility as Christians to help one another, and that I would like them to know more about my Savior, my Lord, and his compassion for them. We talked a long time about Jesus and his love and why he came to the earth. I told them that Jesus taught us how we should help others and we could not just pass by when people need help even though it might have been difficult to obtain. I spoke to them through my translator Victor, and then someone else translated into the Embera language about how they to could be recipients of the grace of God through Jesus Christ our Lord. They wanted to know more, so we talked about salvation. After much conversation, I asked them about a commitment to Jesus Christ, but they wanted to talk more and learn more before taking this step. It came time for my departure, and I hugged Nora, not knowing if I would ever see her again.

I am an emotional person, and sometimes, I cannot contain my feelings. I had come very close to her and her family, especially after having an opportunity to visit in their home in their community. God loves all people and expects us to share that which we have, and I expressed this to them, urging them to please remember all we had talked about and to know I love them and wanted to visit again at some future time. I departed their house with a child holding on to each one of my hands. With my police escort, we made our way back down to the river.

Arriving back at our boat, we made a very important discovery. We did not have enough gas for the return trip. I asked how much gas was needed. "About five more gallons" was the reply. We are deep in the rain forest, and I looked around and at Victor and asked jokingly, "Victor, do you see any gas stations around?" Victor was not too happy because this was his first trip even though he had lived all his life in Panama. The police spoke to some of the people living in the village because there were a number of other piraguas lined up on the bank, each one having an outboard motor, which meant, somebody has some gasoline. I also knew that if we were able to find extra gas, it was not going to be cheap. I was not overly concerned; however, I was responsible for those who volunteered to travel with me on this adventure. At that moment, one of the locals came up with a five-gallon can of gasoline already having the oil mixed in it. Everyone knew what we had done for and was ready to help us out of our predicament. The man would only accept money to cover the gasoline we had received. With our boat fueled and ready for the return trip, we headed back upriver, traveling against the current, which made the trip somewhat slower. The sun was very hot, and I continued reaching into the river, wetting my arms and neck, trying to cool them. It was almost dark when we saw the lights of the town. We pulled up to the bank at the police station and unloaded our boat. I was immediately faced with another problem. We had paid a local driver from the town of Metetí who had the proper truck equipped with four-wheel drive and big mud tires to take us the twenty miles to the community of Sanson. That transit took us over two hours because the road was almost nonexistent. We had told him to be back at a certain time, and he had not arrived, so we waited at the police station. He did arrive about an hour after dark, and we started our mud ride back to Sanson. The driver was very good maneuvering his truck in this type of road. I would have to say there was no road because it was truly a mud ride. If I had not been so exhausted, I would have enjoyed the ride.

On the return trip my thoughts continued to be with all the events of the day. There were challenges on my trip to visit Nora, some almost taking me to the brink of exhaustion, but I truly got more back than I gave when I saw how happy it made each person in that village that this gringo would travel that far to visit them. It meant so much to them for me to sit in their house and to enjoy their hospitality. Their hospitality consisted of some coffee made from the river water loaded with sugar. A hammock for me to rest in was provided. In their way of thinking, what more could a person desire? I learned so much on this trip because they were as interested in me as I was in them. They asked me about life in the United States. "What does the United States look like?" they asked. I tried to explain Atlanta, Georgia, and all of its streets and interstate highways. They wanted to know so much about my house, my family. I showed them pictures of our grandchildren. They passed them around and smiled. One replied to me, "Maybe one day I will visit the United States." He said that in English. "Where did you learn English from?" I asked. I learned they all know a little by studying in school. There is a school in every community, and most students are taught English.

It delighted me to spend time with these sweet people. As I returned to where I would spend the night, my mind went back to my lying in that hammock and enjoying the peacefulness of their beautiful village. It was a beautiful village. It was their home, and they shared what they had with this gringo with the white hair.

Since that day, I have not returned to visit Nora and her family but have often wondered how they were doing. I do have plans on returning soon for it just seems like the simplicity of their lifestyle pulls me back into the deep rain forest. I let them know before I departed that God has blessed me more than I deserve and one of the greatest blessings I had received in recent time was the opportunity he gave me to visit their village.

THE GIFT OF EGGS

A very pretty fourteen-year-old with her arm held very high walked into our clinic with her father. I saw her standing in the line and decided to find out why she could not lower her arm. It has always been my position to check on people who stood in the lines and waited their turn to see one of our doctors or nurses if there seemed to be a serious problem. Some of the people come for medicine. Even though they may not be sick now, they know this might be the only opportunity to obtain pain medicine, vitamins, and the like. So they come and wait even though they're not sick.

I noticed this teenage girl not being able to lower her arm. It brought me great concern seeing she was in a lot of pain. I had a translator inform the others who were ahead of her that she would be moved to the head of the line. No one got angry about this but agreed this was okay. One of our nurses examined her, finding a very large cyst the size of a baseball under her left armpit. After talking with her father, I discovered this family had sixteen children and had no resources to take her to a local clinic or to Panama City. According to him, he thought it would eventually go away by itself, so nothing was done. When he heard there would be a medical team in their community, the first ever, he decided to bring her, allowing the doctors to look at her.

We had a young Panamanian doctor assigned to us by the district director. We learned very quickly she was very efficient.

This young doctor also learned very quickly that our dentist, Dr. Jerry Galloway, never ran out of jokes and had the ability to keep people laughing. Every time she got a break, he wanted to know if she was going to give him an examination. Jerry is very tall, and she would tell him she did not have a table long enough for the examination. That did not deter Dr. Galloway from his insistence that she examine him. Joy, his wife, is very short and has to tell Jerry to back off for a while, but that's like telling a dog not to take the bone.

This young doctor gave our group a tremendous compliment. She said that when she was told she had to work with an American medical team from a church in the United States, we would immediately begin trying to push our religion on her. By the end of the week, she told us she had never had so much fun and had never laughed so much and was so happy to have had the experience of being with us. We all learn from one another and strive always to encourage one another to help others. Jerry never ceased nor ran out of jokes, and he never stopped laughing. Even though the Panamanians did not know what he was saying, they all laughed.

The doctor begins her examination and finds this cyst needs to be drained, and it was not going to be easy and would be very painful. She emphasized to the father that this has to be done or she could die from infection. With a makeshift bed, she is stretched out and prepared for the surgery. Our medical team was working to the west of the town of Torti in the community of Platinilla. This community was surrounded by mountains of extraordinary beauty. You could hear the monkeys hollering and see them in the trees very close to the school where we were working. It was not a place one would think about setting up an operating room and do what we were about to do. One of the nurses very efficiently cleans under her arm, using a solution to kill all germs and limit the possibility of future infection brought on by operating in these conditions. Using lidocaine, she began to make injections around this cyst. I asked the doctor if this was going to be extremely painful. She explained to me that a cyst like this had what was called a core, and she had to get this core out or this cyst would return. She said this was going to be very painful, but it was something necessary. I learned that injecting into areas like this, lidocaine often did no good because the infection would dilute the medicine, making it ineffective. After a number of injections, the doctor makes a small incision to begin the draining process and also to see how much pain she would experience. She did not seem to be in any discomfort, but that was soon to change. Several of us were in the room to lend assistance for we were told we would need to hold her down in order to complete the operation. A lot of infection was drained initially, and then she began to cry when the doctor started mashing around the area, attempting to force out any other infection inside the armpit. Her cries turned into screams. Her father had her arms pulled straight out over her head while I was lying literally across her knees, holding her legs down. A nurse was lying across her midsection while the doctor continued the operation. I finally could not take it any more and asked the doctor about giving another injection. She informed me it would do no good. I asked her how long it was going to take. She said possibly another fifteen minutes. I did not know if I could last fifteen minutes with the screams. I tried to turn away and looked out the door but could not block out the screams. The doctor was digging with a long Q-tip for the core of the cyst. She finally had everything cleaned out to her satisfaction and stitched up the area. Everyone was bathed in sweat with the patient totally wet and everyone else exhausted. This was my first experience in this type of medicine. The doctor explained to me that she would have much better days ahead even though there was a lot of pain experienced. She also assured me this young lady would make a full recovery, and there was no infection left to cause problems later on.

After we got her up and gave her some water and some crackers to help calm her stomach, I inquired as to where they lived. They gave me the same reply I hear so many times, "Not far from here." I learned that "Not far from here" does not always mean not far from here, especially when you're walking. I told her I would visit before I went home to find out how she was doing for I was genuinely concerned about her. On Wednesday morning, I got up and decided this would be the day I would visit her home. We found someone who knew where they lived, and with our backpacks and water and a little food, we started off on this adventure. We walked up and down for a long way on what I would consider a mountain but the locals considered a small hill. We came to a small river, which we would call a creek, and waded across it. After a small amount of time, we came to another river, which we found out was the same one we had just crossed for it had simply doubled back. After about another mile and about the third hour, we came to still another river, which I learned was a different one but was wider and deeper. I was already wet, so getting wetter did not matter. We finally came to this hut in the middle of a large stand of trees. Hearing chickens cackling, I knew we had arrived at our destination. The first thing I saw was the young lady who had received the operation trying to catch a chicken. She was elated to see us.

I do not believe her family really thought I would come. I have always tried to fulfill a promise made to anyone even if sometimes it is a little difficult. This was further than I had anticipated but found the walk extraordinarily beautiful through the mountains. Most of what I saw was something I had read about or seen on television. It was not unusual to see monkeys or parakeets and so many other birds and butterflies by the hundreds. Yes, it was extraordinary. There are hundreds of specimens of birds, and people come from all over the world to bird-watch in Panama. I was getting to see what so many pay thousands of dollars to witness.

Her mother prepared some local bread called hojaldres. This is a fried bread made usually the night before. It is allowed to rise and then shaped with the hand and dropped into grease to fry. It is what I call signature bread from Panama. It usually is the bread the poor eat for it is very cheap to make. If one travels to Panama City much, they will fall in love with this bread.

We sat around eating bread and drinking coffee and having one of the best times of my life. I took time to look at where the incision had been made and to make sure nothing was infected as I have been instructed to do so by the doctor. I asked her if she was in any kind of pain. She replied, "A little bit." Her mother explained to me that this was the first time in a long time her daughter had smiled. It was also the first time she had been outside to do anything for she had been in so much pain. I can only imagine what she had been going through over the past few months.

It makes my heart swell and makes tears come to my eyes when I think about how much pain our medical teams have been able to relieve. Medical people take time off from their jobs and use their personal vacation time and often pay for their own expenses to help people they do not know.

This family had no money, so when I got ready to leave, they gave me a bag of eggs. I did not refuse the gift for I knew it was from the heart and it was their desire to give something in return. We all got together and prayed, and I thanked them for their hospitality. After all the pain this child had gone through over the past thirty-six hours, to see her now feeling good enough to catch a chicken truly warmed my heart. This made all the efforts worthwhile.

A BEAUTIFUL SMILE

When I first met Omaira Campos she was sitting in her wheelchair with the most beautiful smile I have ever seen.

After having completed worship service, the local preacher, Deidel Metrie, in the community of El Tirao asked me to go with him to visit a sister, a Christian lady, not far from the church building. He simply said "She cannot come for she is in a wheelchair." Parking at the road because of muddy conditions, we walked about a quarter of a mile to her mother's house. As I approached her house, I had to bend over so as not to cut my head on the roof, which was very low. As I entered, I saw this beautiful lady with the most gorgeous smile sitting there looking at me. This was my first meeting with Omaira Campos, a thirty-seven-year-old paraplegic. She had been in an automobile accident when she was fifteen years old, which left her paralyzed from the waist down. She had beautiful long coal-black hair that was combed to silk. She had large earrings and red lipstick. Never would I find her without her lipstick, earrings, and looking so beautiful. I sat down, and we became instant friends. I found it very difficult to leave because she was so positive when she didn't have much to be positive about. She did not talk about the accident nor did she talk about not being able to walk and do all the things that everybody enjoys doing. She did not talk about not having a beautiful house or other gadgets that fill our lives.

What she enjoyed the most was conversation. We would sing sometimes only in English if there was not enough to sing in Spanish, and she loved it. When God gave out talents, singing was not one of mine, but she did not care whether I was in tune or not; she just liked to hear the songs even though she did not understand a word.

I promised her I would never come to Panama without stopping for a visit to pray, to sing, and to enjoy conversation with her. She was always waiting, and somehow, she always knew when I would be in the area. We always brought her some items for hygiene, such as toothpaste, soap, and shampoo, for she had little money to buy such things. When a group would come, we always stopped our bus down the road, and the entire group would walk to her house. We would have a devotional, and she loved it. She just brightened up when we walked in.

Every year at Christmas, before departed Panama, we always had a Christmas party in Panama City. We invited the local people to come to enjoy time with us. I asked Omaira if she would like to come to the party. She was elated to have been asked but replied, "How am I going to get there?" She was excited about having the opportunity to get out and go somewhere for it had been a long time since she had left her home. The local preacher picked her up, putting her in his car, and brought her to Panama City with her aunt who would help care for her. The day arrived for the party and so did Omaira. We got her checked into her hotel room. She was then wheeled out around the swimming pool as we gave her a tour of this beautiful hotel.

The time for the party arrived, and the room was full with over 150 people there. We had a special surprise for all the children. They each received a backpack full of goodies for school and for fun.

Ambassador Linda Watt had accepted my invitation to come and be part of this great gathering. The ambassador arrived with her secretary and security and was ushered into our meeting room to the surprise of all of these wonderful people. Most of the people in attendance were poor, and just being there was a treat for them. We just wanted to show them a good time at Christmas. I introduced the ambassador to every table to meet all the people for she liked this the most—meeting people. The last table we came to was the table where Omaira was seated.

Ambassador Watt spent a lot of time talking to her, finding out she lived in Darién. Darién was one of the ambassador's favorite places in Panama. She enjoyed visiting there and traveled there often. She tells Omaira, "The next time I visit Darién, I will visit with you in your home." She told me later how special it made her feel to have someone so important sitting in her home talking to her. She said, "The ambassador acted as though I was important." I told her, "Omaira, you are important, and I am sure Ambassador Watt feels the same way."

No one would believe someone like the Ambassador would take the time to visit such a poor person as Omaira. However, they did not know Ambassador Linda Watt the way I did. Everyone thought she had much more important things to do and never really seriously entertained the idea of taking the time to stop and visit. A few months went by, and one day, I received a phone call from the ambassador's secretary stating that Ambassador Watt was going to visit Darién and wanted to fulfill her promise to call upon Omaira and needed directions on how to find her house. I put her in touch with someone who could direct them.

Upon my next visit to Panama, I stopped to visit with Omaira. The first thing I said to her was "Tell me about your visit with the ambassador." With that big smile and with all her energy, she said to me, "Twenty cars pulled up in my yard." I learned later that twenty cars were not there; however, there were a few traveling with the ambassador. Ambassador Watt told me later she spent about forty minutes visiting in the home of Omaira and later speaking on the radio program *Voice of the Frontier*. The highlight of her whole trip into Darién was the visit with Omaira.

I returned to Panama with a medical team not far from where Omaira lived to work with the Embera Indians. It was my intention to stop by her home for a devotional and spend some time there, as we always did. The weather was getting bad, and it began to rain. I was concerned about this big bus we had might get stuck, so I did not stop even for a moment. It was my intention to return in a smaller vehicle later in the week. I found out later that she kept asking her mother when the Americans are going to come.

The next day, someone runs up to me and says, "The cripple lady from the Darién died today." I could not say anything for I was totally dumbfounded. I said, "You mean Omaira?" He replied, "Yes, she died this morning very suddenly." I ran to my vehicle and called out for a translator and headed for Darién, which was about forty-five minutes from where we were. I arrived at her home, and even before I got to the house, I heard her mother crying loudly, and tears began to stream down my face. I kept saying to myself, "Why did I not take the time to visit yesterday?" I run into the house, and her mother meets me and grabs me, saying in Spanish, "She asked for you and wanted to know when you were coming." I could not speak for it was so sudden she had died. She did not, according to her mother, seem sick. She just died. I went into her room and found her lying there so peaceably. I could only think about how I was going to miss that beautiful smile. I sat down beside her bed and wept, holding her hand, knowing now she was in paradise. I got up and went into the kitchen, taking her mother in my arms, and said, " Omaira is walking around in heaven on her own two legs. She is now charming everyone with that beautiful smile." We then had a prayer together. I assured her mother we would help where we could.

Every time I pass by her house, I think of all the wonderful times we had together; however, I also think of her walking around in heaven with that beautiful smile, singing the beautiful songs around the throne of God. She brought so much joy to each one of us and made us all think about the blessings that come our way and how we never look up and say thank you to God. Omaira taught everyone who visited her that life is beautiful, and she cherished every moment, longing for the next visit.

Ambassador Linda Watt wrote an article in memory of Omaira:

> I first met Omaira Campos at a Christmas party hosted by Panama Missions. It was an event the like of which I have seldom encountered. The children were excited and dressed in their holiday best, the moms and dads were enjoying what to them must have been a scene they could hardly imagine: a nice hotel, Christmas boxes packed with thoughtfully selected gifts, a delicious feast, and the spirit of fun and love on the part of all the Americans and Panamanians present. But Larry had a special treat for me. "Linda," he said," you have to meet Omaira!" And he introduced me to a beautiful woman, in a wheelchair with a smile that would light up fifth Avenue. Omaira had been hit by a car a number of years ago when she was a teenager and had never walked again. Before she met the Panama Missions folks, she had been totally housebound. The wheelchair that Larry got for her truly set her free. Now she could attend church in her small town of El Tirao, Darién Province just beyond Torti. She could participate much more actively in the life of her community.
>
> I visited Omaira in June on my last trip to Darién before leaving Panama. Having the American ambassador show up in a tiny village causes quite a stir as you can imagine. We parked the car and walk down a bumpy path to Omaira's house reminding me Larry said he was going to try on his next trip to build her a proper sidewalk to

make her wheelchair more maneuverable. When I got to her house, Omaira greeted me with that million-dollar smile and we talked a few minutes and visited with her family. I took a few gifts such as shampoo and the like. But we left with so much more! She insisted that we accept gifts of food from the garden and some goodies she had made but most of all we took with us the memory of a person who has nothing by our standards but whose heart is enormous and whose faith is strong.

The next day in a radio interview in Metetí I talked about Omaira and how inspiring she was. I hope she was listening. I think she would have love to hear her name on the radio.

When I heard that she had passed away I wondered what would've happened had she lived closer to medical care. I know that paraplegics face special medical risk and of course I don't know what her condition really was. But in her community and in other isolated communities in that area if you have a serious accident it is highly unlikely you'll receive adequate medical treatment. Perhaps through Panama Missions they will find a remedy by building a modern new clinic in the area. But then all of this I will be thinking of Omaira. I know should be standing in heaven smiling down on us.

Linda E. Watt
US Ambassador to Panama, December 2002–July 2005

HOW ARE YOU?

The first time I saw Johnny Gonzolas he was sitting in his wheelchair under the trees not saying anything to anyone just watching all that was going on.

He was there every day, watching the work that was going on at the church building in Santa Fe.

Santa Fe, Darién, is a small town located about 140 miles southeast of Panama City, Panama, off the main highway about 2 miles to the west. The church building is on the main road and is the first building you see as you enter the town.

I had not met Johnny but had known his mother, who was a member of this church. Johnny was not a Christian, but that did not mean he was a bad man. He just never had seen the need for Jesus even after he injured himself in a car accident that left him paralyzed in every part of his body with the exception of his left arm. Everyone in the area new Johnny, so there was always someone to push his wheelchair wherever he needed to go.

I asked Johnny if he would like to come into the church building. When he replied yes, before worship service started, a couple of people would pick his wheelchair up and place it in the church building. He always sat in the back of the building as though he was embarrassed to go toward the front. Our entire group took to Johnny, trying to help him be more comfortable. He had learned a few words of English, like "How are you?" Every day he would say the same thing. "How are you?" He was learning a few words so that he could communicate with the Americans, he said. I asked him where he lived. He said he lived over two hours from Santa Fe. He and his mother came to town on Saturday so that they could be in church on Sunday. Toward the end of the revival, I knew Johnny had not become a Christian. Johnny knew what he needed to do but was afraid because being in a wheelchair, it would be difficult for him to be baptized. We all told him that several men would be around him to take him into the water to baptize him. On the last night, Johnny was in the back of the building when he rolled his wheelchair to the front, indicating that he wanted to be a Christian.

Because of an illness, I was unable to participate in his baptism but went down to the river as four men picked up his wheelchair and carried him into the river, baptizing him into Jesus Christ. Johnny changed after that and became a happy man who loved to be around people, and above all, he loved to be around the North American people, trying to learn the language, always asking, "How are you?"

On the last day, we were asked to go to a small community that was unable to come into Santa Fe for the medical, which would require over a two-hour walk through the jungle. We departed early the next morning for this community. We drove our four-wheel drives as far as we could, and then everyone picked up a box of medicine and equipment and walked for over two hours. When we got there, there were not a lot of people, but there was one house where people came to be cared for. This was the house of Johnny. The man who had asked us to come said, "I wanted you all to come here so you can see what Johnny has to go through just to get to church every Sunday." They would put Johnny on a stretcher, and two men would carry him all the way to Santa Fe. They then put him in his wheelchair and pushed him to the meeting house. I would have to say that this was commitment to Jesus Christ. That is commitment to one's faith, and I do not believe we even understand nor do we have to go through such to go to worship service. Johnny never missed worship. He looked forward to Sundays because this was the part of his week when he could come and be with others. The members always cooked a meal at their church building for those who were unable to return home. The church was a family, and they loved one another, and they loved Johnny.

Johnny somehow would get the birthdays of the North Americans, and by selling newspapers for a nickel outside a store in Santa Fe, he would get enough money to buy a little time on his cell phone. When someone's birthday came up, he would call the United States. This was his conversation: "Happy birthday, Larry. How are you? Bye." That was just about the gist of his conversation.

A man by the name of Larry English fell in love with this simple man and sends him at special times during the year a little money to help him out. Sometimes people can change lives not by what they have but by simply being there. Johnny continues to live in Santa Fe and now has moved into the town because his health is declining. Those of us who know him are better people because Johnny came into our lives. Perhaps each one of us needs a Johnny to keep us from feeling so sorry for ourselves when things do not go our way or when we do not get what we want.

The following is a note from Larry English regarding his very special friend Johnny:

> I met a young man in Santa Fe, Johnny Gonzolas; he was about thirty-five years old. He was a quadriplegic because of a car accident when he was about twenty. Johnny is totally dependent on others for everything. He gets no government assistance of any kind. His dear mother, his son, and relatives take care of him. When I first met him, he told me he lived back in the jungle but went to church every Sunday. On Saturdays, his son and several relatives

would tie a hammock to a pole, place him in it, and carry him several miles through the jungle to a road. There they will wait an unknown amount of time for a ride into the little town of Santa Fe so they could go to church on Sunday. Sunday night, they reversed the process. Johnny has struggles that I will never comprehend. On our birthdays, my wife, my son, and myself receive a call to wish us a happy birthday. He has never forgotten. What a lesson in humility.

Johnny truly has made his impact upon the lives of us all, and he does not realize the impact he has made. Most times when I arrive and Johnny is sitting there in the shade of a tree, he would say "How is my brother Larry English?" He never forgets those who have befriended him. Johnny's health has begun to deteriorate, and only God knows the future, but we know God has the future in his hands. The word that Larry English wrote about a lesson in humility is most definitely true of Johnny for he taught us so much. A lesson I think we learned from Johnny is those who have so little often do more with what they have than those of us who are blessed beyond measure. One year, when we were collecting items to sell at our annual fund-raising dinner, Johnny hears of this project. Selling papers in front of a store in Santa Fe, he takes a nickel from the sale of each paper and saves it until he has enough money to purchase a beautiful carved statue of a parakeet. He gives me the carving as his contribution to the mission work in his area. Never think yourself so arrogant that you cannot learn from people like Johnny, who often are so insignificant to those around him, but he makes his impact upon the hearts of those who know him.

ALTO DE LA PLAYON

After visiting the Embera community of Alto de la Playon and having seen their gardens, I got the idea I would use my expertise in planting them a garden. I had been successful in Alabama and decided this would be a good thing to do. Little did I know the challenges of planting a garden in the tropics. I told folks I had planted gardens before and it could not be much different in Panama. That statement would come back to haunt me. Not only was it different, it was also funny to watch the Indians use a tiller. But first, let me tell you how it came about for us to decide we would plant gardens.

I was visiting in the village of Alto de Playon, about a fifteen-minute boat ride up the Chucunaque River. This village was composed of refugees from Columbia who had fled from the situations regarding the rebel groups there. They had so very little because they left with nothing and walked all the way across the Darién rain forest, living under very difficult circumstances with very little food and bad water. I went to a large store about fifty miles away in the town of Torti and purchased a lot of food composed of rice, beans, flour, cooking oil, sugar, salt, coffee, and some high-protein milk for the babies. When we arrived back, our boats were filled, and the people were excited and began to help us unload. We gave each family enough food for approximately two weeks, but this was a short-term fix. I walked throughout the village, looking at how we might be able to help them on a long-term basis. I noticed behind some of the houses there was a field about two acres in size. I discussed with the village chief what he thought about planting some crops if we help them with the seeds. He thought this to be a fantastic idea. On the November container, we had shipped in two new garden tillers, so I decided we would bring them here and till up this field. This was a bigger undertaking than I had thought. However, we were up for the task and began tilling up all this ground. I thought it would be a lot of fun to allow the local people to try their hand at tilling. If you have ever used a tiller, you will know it is not easy, especially when new ground is being worked. I turned my tiller over to the chief, showing him how to press down the lever, and, through my translator, told him to make sure he held on. He pushed down the lever, and the tiller immediately jerked him off his feet, but he did not let go of the tiller. He managed to regain his footing, but the tiller was going around in circles, dragging him, and he still refused to let it go. We all began to laugh as we watched him operate this machine or rather the machine operate him. He finally got semi control of the machine and learned how to maneuver it. One has to know that you do not allow a tiller to maneuver the operator because you very quickly will become exhausted when trying to hold the tiller back. Everyone tried their hand at the tiller and actually enjoyed the work. After working all day, we managed to get the land broken up and ready for planting the next day. There was one small problem. We did not have any fertilizer. Back over on the mainland, there was a cattleman who had some very large piles of cow manure. He allowed us to have all we wanted, so we purchased some large cloth bags and filled them up with the manure. Going back, we had two boats full of cow manure. Arriving back in the village, the locals helped carry it to the field. We then spread it out over the entire garden spot and then tilled it in. After this, we then laid off the rows for planting. We planted corn, carrots, cucumbers, watermelons, pepper, and tomatoes. We stood back and looked at what God had done; after that, we all got together and prayed, thanking him for allowing us to be part of this work.

While all the work was going on in the garden, we had a group of young people holding Vacation Bible School with the many children that were about. Periodically, they would come out and look and see how things were going. What a tremendous time we had. We now stood back and waited for the rains, knowing God would give the increase. I returned the following month to check on how the crops were doing. By this time, there were vines on the cucumbers. The corn was waist-high, and in general, the crops were doing fantastic. People feel so much better when they can be part of the solution. I told them how they could save seeds for next year. They were eager to learn and were very appreciative of all we were doing.

I remember a phrase from President Ronald Reagan, "Give a man a fish and he has fish for today, but teach a man to fish and he has fish for life." It was our goal to teach them how to do for themselves, and we found out they had much rather work than have everything given to them. We began to teach them how they could make compost bins so they would have fertilizer year by year. The driving factor for all we were doing was hunger. The people were hungry for something more than just a banana or plantain or occasional fish. We wanted to help them obtain some of those things. The idea of teaching people how to farm is not a new one and is being done all over the world. It is a very effective way of eliminating hunger.

The world's hunger rate is out of hand with millions dying of starvation each year while governments sit by and do nothing other than fight. The poor get caught in the middle and are often used as pawns. We have all seen the scenes on television of the widespread starvation around the world. When Jesus saw these scenes, it broke his heart. Remember his words, "As you have done it to the least of these." "The least of these" meant the poor, the downtrodden, the forsaken. We may not be able to eliminate all of the hunger around the world, but that does not mean we should not help someone somewhere. Help one person at a time, one village at a time.

Remember what Paul wrote in 1 Corinthians 3:5–7: "I have planted, Apollos watered, but God gave the increase. So then neither he who plants is anything, nor he who waters, but God who gives the increase. Now he who plants and he who waters are one and each will receive his own reward according to his own labor. For we are *laborers together with God*." We plant and God will take care of the rest. You and I are in partnership with God. Friend, you may never travel outside your community, but there are neighbors who might need help albeit temporary. As a Christian, never make the mistake of saying there is nothing you can do. There is something all can do. All you need to do is take a look around.

Someone asked my father why he planted so much in his garden when he knew our family did not need all of it. His reply, "I like to give things away. I just like to watch things grow." We were poor but always had food to share. This is a lesson I teach even as we planted the gardens. Share! Just because one is poor is no excuse for not sharing the increase. I spoke to the poor of Panama about the liberality of the Macedonians. Note the words from Paul:

> Moreover, brethren, we make known to you the grace of God that has been given to the churches of Macedonia that in a great trial of affliction, the abundance of their joy and *their deep poverty*, abounded in the riches of their liberality. For I testify that according to *their* ability, yes, and beyond *their* ability *they gave* of their own accord, begging us with much urgency that we would receive the gift and the fellowship of the ministering to the saints.
>
> 2 Corinthians 8:1–3, ASV

What made the Macedonians' contribution exceptional was the fact that they gave out of an economic situation that was very difficult. Though the times were hard for them, they still gave to the need of others. They gave with a joyful spirit. It was not a grudging gift. They were poor churches (people), yet they did not use their poverty as an excuse not to give. Too often, poor churches complain about their economic situation, and thus, they neglect to manifest the spirit of giving what they have. However, those churches that realize the tremendous gift of grace God has given to them and the eternal glory that is yet to come will give out of their poverty. The spirit of giving is based on the concepts that Jesus taught on giving. Since we have freely received God's gifts, freely we should give to others. In Matthew 10:8, Jesus told the disciples, "Freely you have received, freely give." If we violate this principle, then we will not grow spiritually in favor with God nor will God look favorably upon us as Christians if we do not sacrificially contribute to the misfortune of others.

A WHEELCHAIR FOR MOTHER

She was lying there on the floor of her house with only a wraparound cloth around her waist. Flies were on her lips and were flying all around her. I reached over and drove the flies away and helped her sit up. She just looked at me. There was no pillow or even something soft for her to get comfortable, just a wood floor. I spoke to her in my broken Spanish, asking her how she was doing. I was just trying to make conversation but only received a blank stare. I thought she might be deaf but found out she only understood the Embera dialect. I reached over and combed her hair back, feeling the need to do something. She looked so miserable. What could I do? How could I help? These were questions I asked her son who was standing there.

I thought back to my own mother as I stood there looking at her. My mother lived in a comfortable apartment in a retirement center the last years of her life. The people of the village loved this little lady but had no resources or connections to get anything she needed to make her more comfortable, so they did what they could for her. She had not been out of the village in many years, having lost the ability to walk. She had not one single comfort in her life, not even as she came to the end.

In the United States, we do everything we can to make our senior citizens comfortable in their last years. Whatever they need, we try to make sure they have it. A comfortable bed, decent clothes, enough food, and clean water are provided. Her family was doing all they could with the resources they had. She finally smiled at me and tried to rise up by herself. Again, I spoke to her in Spanish, broken as it is, and said, "Good morning, Grandmother! How are you?" Her son translated, and she replied, "Fine!" I found out she did understand some basic phrases of Spanish. I could barely hear her speak. Her son was standing next to me as I tried to carry on this conversation. I was really surprised she understood Spanish because most of the older people only speak Embera. She had lived in Panama for over fifty years and, through the natural course of things, learned some Spanish. I stood there not saying anything to anyone but could not stop the tears that came to my eyes as I watched this sweet little lady just lie there on the wooden floor, and the flies continued landing on her lips and her ears as she did not have the strength to brush them off. Again, I took my hand and stroked it through her hair and thought that at the end of one's life, they should enjoy some form of comfort.

I turned away to walk through the rest of the village, which was very small having been relocated after the floods of 2010. As you approach this village from the river, you look up the hill, which stands several hundred feet above the bank of the river. The people had dug out some footholds, making it easier to go and come from the river. It was from the river they get their water, take their baths, and wash their clothes. It was difficult for this gringo to climb that mountain. More on this later!

I have taken a number of other people to visit this little lady, and they too, like me, were moved. Her son said to me, "My mother was born February 5, 1905." I looked at him and said, "That makes her 105 years old." I had to tell others about her for I found it so remarkable that someone so old could survive the elements. I found out she was the second oldest living person in Panama. At least that's what I was told.

Her son came up to me and asked, "Do you think it is possible to get my mother a wheelchair?" I immediately said, "I think that would be possible."

Being this far upriver, normally you do not have any cell phone signal, but I thought I would try because we were standing so high above the river on this mountain. I discovered I did have a cell phone signal. I immediately called my good friend Tom Ford, president of the Gift of Life Foundation in Panama City. He also is the one in charge of distribution of wheelchairs for the Wheelchair Foundation. He answers the phone as he always does, "How is Larry doing today?" I said to him, "I am doing wonderful, Tom, but you will never believe what I'm about to tell you and where I am calling you from. I am standing here in the middle of the rain forest on the Chucunaque River in an Embera village. I have just met the second oldest person in Panama according to her son. She is 105 years old. She is lying here on the floor of her house, not able to go anywhere or even get around the village without someone carrying her. Do you have any available wheelchairs?" His reply to me was, "You know you can get a wheelchair anytime you need it."

Tom and I have been working together, swapping resources, helping people together ever since we were introduced by Ambassador Linda Watt in 2003. We have grown to love each other and each other's mission. "When do you want the wheelchair" he replied. I told him I would like to get it on my next trip into Panama City, which would be in a day or two, so we could deliver it to her before I returned to the United States. I have always been of the mentality that when someone needs help, they do not need it next year. If you're going to help someone, go ahead and do it now while they need it. If you're hungry, you are hungry now not next week. I told her son she would have a wheelchair by week's end. He looked over his shoulder and said to the people who were gathered there waiting on the answer,

"Mama is going to get her wheelchair this week." They all began to clap. I later told Tom I wish he had been with me to see the elation of the village knowing grandmother was going to get a wheelchair soon.

I departed the village for the one-hour trip upriver, going directly back to our clinic to make plans for when I would go back to Panama City to get the wheelchair. I rose early the next day, departing for the four-hour drive to Panama City. I go directly to Tom Ford's office to pick up the wheelchair that was still in the box. It was a beautiful red wheelchair that was going to bring so much happiness to these simple people. I decided I would not wait any longer but traveled back to Darién and arriving in the night. The next morning, I was up early for I almost could not contain myself. It was going to be an exciting time, I felt, to deliver this wheelchair. From our clinic to the river, it is about forty-five minutes because part of trip is over a dirt road, which really is more like a trail, and is only accessible when it has not rained very much. When I arrived, there was a piragua (dugout) waiting to take me back downriver to the village. Arriving at the village, some of the family came down to help unload the boat, which also had other items they would need, such as rice, oil, flour, and beans. Today, not only did we deliver the wheelchair but we brought clean water to this village as well.

Some of the young people thought it necessary to help this gringo get to the top of hill. They thought this was funny because I had to stop several times to rest. I found me a pole that provided some security to keep me from falling. One thing I have always enjoyed was putting on like I was more tired than I am or was about to starve to death. The Indians like me carrying on like this. As a matter of fact, it has become the way I am, and they all like it. That is, I never get serious about anything unless there's something to get serious about. I even asked them one time which way they would like me to be, serious never smiling, or never serious so we can all do a lot of laughing. Everybody said the latter. We like to laugh and have fun.

I make it to the top of the hill with others carrying the wheelchair and the other items. There is a large crowd assembled. I stop putting my hands on my knees; I poke my tongue out like I could hardly breathe. They are laughing, and I make a big deal out of the children who thought they were helping me up the hill.

We go directly to Grandmother's house. She is still lying in the same place as before. Some of her family put some clothes on her for the occasion of presenting the wheelchair. I opened up the wheelchair, put the footrest on it, and everybody is elated for the son tells me later they thought it was going to be a long time before they got the wheelchair. They never thought it would come so soon. I let them know that this is a gift from God and we are here representing God for he expects us to share our blessings with others. I told them this is one of those blessings and we were only too happy to help. Some of the people began to cry tears of joy when grandmother was picked up by her son and placed in the wheelchair. Grandmother looks up at me and holds up her hand, waving at me with a big smile on her face. What a moment of joy it was for this entire family and for this mission. The house is several feet off the ground, so some of her family take the wheelchair with her in it and placed it on the ground. No sooner had it been placed on the ground that some of the great-great-grandchildren surrounded her chair with one of them pushing her throughout the village and with her waving at others as she was wheeled around. What a moment of joy. Family members came up to me and started pumping my hand, thanking me for the wheelchair, for making their mother, grandmother so happy. I said to them, "This is God's blessing. He has blessed us, and you all are receiving a share of the blessings through others." I went on to explain to them where the wheelchair came from. Yes, what a moment of joy, of happiness, of goodwill. Again, I believe this is what Jesus was talking about when he said in Matthew 25, "As you have done it to the least of these my brethren you have done it unto me." As I think about that Scripture and read the words, "the least of these" I think about this 105-year-old lady for this is who Jesus was referring to.

CHRISTMAS ON THE CHUCUNAQUE RIVER

In December of 2010, I arrived in Panama City along with my wife, Betsy, and two others for the purpose of distributing Christmas gifts supplied through Panama Mission's Operation Christmas Joy. We planned to start the distribution process in the Darién Province and had made plans to deliver the Christmas gifts to the villages that were deep in the rain forest all along the Chucunaque and some of the smaller rivers. It was the first time I have had the privilege of traveling this far into the Darién Province. Our plans were to go as far as the town of Boca de Cupe, not far from the border to Columbia. Little did I know how the entire mission was about to be changed, and the gifts would have so much more meaning than they normally would.

The first thing I noticed as we were loading our boats in the town of Yavisa, which is at the end of the Pan-American Highway, was the river was extremely high and very rapid. It looked almost dangerous with so much debris floating down the river, but the boats continued to come in and out of the port, so I left our safety up to the young man who would be driving our boat. The mayor of the Darién Province had furnished a very good fiberglass boat with a seventy-five-horsepower motor for the two-day trip downriver. All the Christmas gifts were loaded in two piraguas and all the people in the larger boats.

We started out and had not gone very far when it was determined that one of the piraguas was too small to carry such a heavy load, especially with the river running so high and so rapid; therefore, we waited for another larger piragua to arrive, so we pulled into a small community to wait. As we waited we noticed there were a number of houses located in this community with water standing all around them.

We took the opportunity to give some candy and other treats to the children standing around to see what these gringos were all about. We finally continued our trip. The Chucunaque River is the longest river in Panama, and during the height of the rainy season, it is very wide and deep. Many Indian villages line the river, and most were flooded out as well as all of their crops. Even the mayor of this area was not aware of the extreme flooding we were finding and the despair of the people. It did not take me very long to realize that we had to do more than just give out Christmas gifts.

Our boat captain was traveling very fast along the river, and I thought at least he would slow down going around some of the bends of the river. Mike Ray and I continue to look at each other, hoping he would slow down, but he did not. Therefore, we just sat back and tried to enjoy the scenery that was flashing by as we traveled deeper into the interior. We finally approach the location of the first village where we plan to begin distributing Christmas gifts. This was a Wounaan Indian community. The children were waiting on the bank of the river as we approached. It was heartbreaking to look through the community and see all of the flooding. We were informed by the local chief that they had lost all their crops. Plantain, rice, and beans—everything was wiped out, he said. Even the fishing was bad because the river was so high. We found hunger everywhere. We unloaded the Christmas gifts from the piragua that had arrived about an hour after we did. It had started to rain again, but this did not deter us from our mission. We were wet and, with all probability, were going to stay that way.

After the distribution of the Christmas gifts, I had a conversation with the village chief about their situation. I looked at the water and asked him if they were drinking the water. He told me they had nothing else, and the people were sick from having to drink bad water. There also was the problem of not having enough food because all the crops were washed away. I visited some of the homes, sitting down with the people, asking them about their situation.

In one village, El Salto, we had difficulty maneuvering our boat up to the bank. Everywhere I looked I saw devastation. When one has so little and the little is lost, what do you do? This was going to be a question that would haunt me over the next several months as we tried to keep them from starving and dying from disease resulting from bad water. As always, water is going to be the key to survival even more so than food. Both were in very short supply. The only water source was the contaminated river. The community had moved to the school, which was a lot higher than the village. Over six hundred people were crowded in to an area of about two acres with makeshift shacks and very little to eat. I went from house to house, talking with the families and trying to encourage them. At one house, I found a family of six living under some old tin with no facilities, no water, and very little food. The mother had a big pot of rice cooking over an open fire. I tried to cheer them up by talking about the Christmas they had enjoyed with gifts supplied by our organization.

It is very difficult to feel happiness when your children are sick and you have so little to feed them. This was my first experience in dealing with people who had been affected by extreme flooding. I found myself having a difficult time holding back my emotions. I put my arms around the children after giving them lollipops and other candies and asking them about school.

I talked to a teenager, asking her how all of this made her feel. The young lady really could not give me an answer, and I do not know if I even expected one. I was actually making small talk, hoping to make them feel better.

In times past, under bad circumstances, we have had people attempt to give us their children to take them to the United States because they knew they would have a better life and have an opportunity they could not provide.

I found in one village a mother with twins and only enough milk in her breast to feed one for she herself was malnourished. I could not just leave and not attempt to do something that would help this mother save both children. I traveled to Meteti, which had a large store, and purchased baby formula and several gallons of pure water so the babies would not get sick drinking contaminated milk. This was not a rare case because so many of the mothers themselves are malnourished with some of them sick with nausea and diarrhea and do not have sufficient breast milk, which leads to a malnourished child. Where does it end? This was a question that would plague me, and I did not know what to do. I stood there on top of this small mountain outside the school, looking at a people who were desperate to survive. Our resources were running very low. All of the local young people I had brought with me gathered all the children in a big circle and began singing and playing games with them even in the rain, trying to take their minds away even for a moment from the difficult situation they were living in. After the games, each child was given a juice box and some cookies as a treat.

On another day with a small group, I traveled farther into the Darién Province toward Columbia and witnessed devastation that would break your heart for the river was far out of its banks with all the crops gone for the year and with no idea when they might be able to replant. I found out that the situation with replanting was even worse than I thought because now they had no seeds for their main staple was plantain, a large green banana, which, when fried or boiled, is very good. These come back every year and do not need to be replanted; however, the floods took care of that, and now, the people have no recourse unless groups like ours came to the rescue. All I could do today along with my good friend Mike Ray was to look at the future and see what we might be able to do with the money we had. We approached the last checkpoint, which said, "Welcome to the Frontier". This was a police checkpoint before one reaches the border to Columbia, and all boats going and coming on the river had to pull in here and have their documents checked. This is one way they control the drug trade and other illegal trade going up and down the river. After a few minutes with the police, we continued on arriving at the town of Boca de Cupe. This town was like so many others on the river with the main street located next to the river. We walked about fifteen minutes to the main police station to report in and let them know there were gringos in town. Very few gringos venture this far into the interior of Darién for obvious reasons. The police captain put two policemen as security with us while we were in town.

We then left and started walking around town. We found there many people, especially elderly and mothers without husbands, suffering terribly from a lack of food and clean water. Again, the question came to me, What are we going to do about the situation with the resources we have?

We had to first attend to the mission today—bringing joy to the children. They lined up on the bank of the river as we distributed the Christmas gifts, which had arrived in our other boats a few minutes earlier. The elation they all felt could be seen as they got their Christmas gifts and immediately began opening them. For many, this was the first Christmas gift they had received. We also had with us several boxes of beautiful diaper bags filled with things a mother needs. Every mother with a baby got a diaper bag until there were no more left.

Some Indians arrived in a motorized piragua to receive the gifts for their village located close to the border of Colombia. The police would not allow us to go any further than Boca de Cupe. We immediately loaded all their Christmas gifts into their piragua so they could depart as soon as possible. The piragua is not known for its speed, so it would take them several hours to return to their village.

It was getting late in the day, close to 4:00 p.m., and we needed to get off the river before dark. I knew we would be pressed to make it back to Yavisa and then on to Sanson before dark. As luck would have it, our boat would not start. It would not be a good idea to spend the night in this town, but it looked like that might happen. The boat operator continued to work on the motor by pulling the plug and doing other things he thought might work. With a small prayer on behalf of the motor, it fired up, so he started backing out, but it quit again. However, luckily, it fired back up, and we finally got under way, traveling as fast as possible against the current and arriving back at our destination around dark.

As soon as we arrived back at the clinic, we began making plans as to how we were going to help the people in this situation. If people are hungry, they do not need to wait months for people to help them. They need help right now, not next week. There is not enough time to get a committee together and debate the issue, as is so often the case. We looked at all the money we had available to us, which was around $2,000. There was a large Chinese store located in the town of Metetí. Early the next morning, we went to this store to find out what we could get with the money we had. I had made friends with the owner of the store and let him know what we wanted to do. He gave me everything at his cost, which allowed our $2,000 to go a lot further.

We had identified quite a few families that were suffering worse than others. These were senior citizens who had no resources and families with small children and especially women without husbands. We were able to prepare enough food for one month for seventy families. This might not seem like much, but we thought we could help the most needy at the time. Wasting no time obtaining a truck to deliver the food to the port, we loaded into our boats and headed back downriver. We stopped periodically at houses along the bank of the river, providing each of them a bag of food. This was totally unexpected for them, and they were elated.

On the trip back down the river, I had with me two policemen as security, not that I felt like I needed them but it was not up to me. Word got out that a gringo was delivering food up and down the river. There were so many families and so little food it broke my heart to pass by a house that needed something, but I knew we had to pick and choose today. I explained everywhere we went that this was a blessing we were sharing so they could have a better Christmas. This was supposed to be a joyous time for it was Christmas time, and what is Christmas when you have nothing to eat?

After the distribution process was complete, our return from Boca de Cupe was uneventful, and all the way back I was trying to decide what we could do on a longer-range plan to help these people. I was overjoyed to hear that two other groups known to me were helping supply the same food items to other villages deep in the Darién that were cut off from the world through the floods. Jesus would have looked out over this devastation with compassion on the people for they were wandering about as sheep having no shepherd. It was in us as Christians to live up to our responsibility and provide where we could and help with what we have in a very difficult situation.

After I returned to our clinic in Sanson, we prayed for these people, asking God to protect them and give us the resources to provide what they needed.

We soon learned our situation was going to get worse before it got better.

We departed the next morning and learned through our driver that the flooding was even worse than we had thought. We were now cut off from getting back into Panama City for the entire area from Chepo to Bayano was underwater. It seemed someone had not been doing his job monitoring the dam, and by the time they saw the problem, the water was close to going over the top. They open all the floodgates, resulting in flooding every community downstream. The town of Canita and Llano were totally flooded. These people had to be evacuated to the town of Torti forty miles to the south and housed at the school.

We decided to go to the school and find out what they needed and found the community of Torti had turned out to feed these people. Here were poor people helping poor people. They were not waiting for others but saw a need and were taking care of the need as best they could. Someone had provided a cow, someone else rice and so many other items needed for the people have left their homes and all of their goods behind. They were told to get on the buses because the floods were coming. The area was flooded and had alligators on top of the houses. It had become a dangerous situation for everyone.

As we approached the school, all we could see were people milling about. I am sure they all were wondering what is to become of their lives. People's entire lives are disrupted, and they do not know about their future. Much of their future, however, depends upon how we, as their neighbors, react.

What if it were me and my family? What if it was your family? As a Christian, we cannot just sit and do nothing. It warms my heart when I see people of all faiths come together, roll up their sleeves, and go to work helping their neighbor. I live in Alabama, where over 250 people were killed and towns devastated and many hundreds injured during the tornadoes of

April 2011. People having lost everything were helping others in the same situation.

As I stood in the school of Torti, Panama, I was moved to tears as I watched neighbor helping neighbor. They did not even know one another before this day, and now it seems they are all family. I watched the people butcher a cow while others were shucking corn, and still others were stirring pots over fires to feed the many people who had no place to go.

In one classroom, a young woman was about to give birth. On the third day, as she lay on the floor on a mat someone had given her to make her more comfortable, she gave birth to her baby. I stood there with the minister of justice of Panama and spoke to this young mother and father. She held a small bundle in her arms not knowing what the future held for them. She says, "Perhaps we do not have a house to go back to. I do not know."

It was getting late in the evening as my small group along with the Christians of the local Church of Christ were discussing what we could do for the children.

We decided to redirect some of the Christmas gifts that were to go to other locations throughout Panama for this is where they were needed today. I knew with these Christmas gifts we could bring a small amount of joy to people who had so little to be joyful about. We went to the local store and purchased juice and cookies for a party for the children. Our group began to get larger as more and more people wanted to participate. We loaded up the Christmas gifts as well many new clothes for children, new dresses made so lovingly by Christian ladies from all over the United States. No one even dreamed about what these new clothes would mean to these people. Loaded with all of these items, we arrived at the school. We had someone announce to have all the children come out into the center of the grounds of the school. There were around one hundred children, so we had enough for everyone. We even had enough of the new clothes to give every child two sets along with underwear, socks, and shoes. At no other time in my ministry had I felt so useful and gratified. I was also very thankful for the many Christians in the United States who worked so hard to help people they did not know. When we left the United States, we had no idea we would be faced with this situation. God used all the things that we sent as a blessing for others.

There's a wonderful old song I love to sing in worship: "There Shall Be Showers of Blessing." It is one of my favorite songs, so I sang it to myself as I thought within my own heart how God put us here on this day to be a blessing to these people.

Imagine every person in the United States who made a gift, made a dress, purchased clothes, or gave money. They did not know this was going to be showers of blessing on this day in December of 2010. The children lined up excited when they saw the stacks of Christmas gifts behind us. The mothers were even more excited when they saw all the new items of clothes being given out. We allowed the mothers to select two sets of clothes for their children. Each time they said, "Thank you for everything." Many were crying for this was all they would have for Christmas. The children were waiting patiently their turn to receive their Christmas gift.

The Christmas gifts that are so lovingly made by Christians all over the United States are the greatest. They are filled to the top. Sometimes they're so full, the top has to be taped. We use a plastic box that cost a dollar because of the tropics and the moisture. One minister said to his congregation as they were preparing for Christmas, "Put your heart in the box." People truly put their hearts in these gifts. I suppose the greatest joy for me was to go around and watch the children as they tear into the gift and see the treasures inside. We watched as they pushed the little cars around in the dirt. Sometimes there are combs and brushes. The girls began combing their hair, even putting in new barrettes that came with the box. Some have new jewelry. Yes, it was such a delight and even more so on this Christmas.

I had with me twelve beautifully made baskets that were in very large bags. Each one of them had a beautiful teddy bear along with other items. As I gave them out, one mother comes to me, begging for the last one. It just melted my heart to have her want this bag so bad. I gave it to her, and my reward was a big hug. Everywhere, people were coming up to us, saying, "Feliz Navidad." (Merry Christmas.)

One individual said to me, "This is the best Christmas of my life." She was one of the helpers handing out the Christmas gifts. She said this was not because she received a Christmas gift but because she was part of being able to hand out the gifts. I think it possibly was one of the greatest Christmases I had spent anywhere because on that night, so much joy was brought to so many.

KEEPING THE MISSION INTERESTING

Keep these words in mind as you read this chapter for this is what makes mission work never dull. During my twenty-nine years of mission work, there have been many humorous things that have happened to me and others. I have always encouraged people to have fun on mission trips, let people see our happiness while witnessing Jesus in our lives. One way to do this is to laugh together. I believe Jesus had a humorous side about him. He was not always serious; I am convinced of that. Perhaps when he was sitting around talking with the disciples, they would tell stories about something that happened along the way. I really encourage Christians to laugh, to have fun, to display a loving relationship. It is through these means that more people will be attracted to what we're trying to teach and that is for them to have that personal one-on-one relationship with their Master.

God wants us to have fun and, yes, laugh. We laugh at ourselves, and we talk about it, so I included some of those humorous things that have happened along the way.

Let me now give you some illustrations, although perhaps humorous, of what it means to build a relationship by participating in activities that might even be outside your comfort zone. Many times, I have been invited into the homes of indigenous people, sitting on a log and sometimes lying in a hammock, enjoying the laughter over a bowl of rice with a piece of chicken. We've always had the joke that we would either have rice and chicken or chicken and rice. I had the opportunity to visit in the home of one Embera Indian family and as I sat there drinking a cup of coffee, they asked me if I would like to go fishing. I told them I would like nothing better but did ask him what kind of fish we would be fishing for. Their reply was tilapia. I love tilapia but had never fished for any for it is a tropical fish. I saw them gather up some nets and head toward the river, which was very close-by. The biggest part of the Embera Indians live on the rivers for their main staple food is fish. We arrived at the river, and they just walked on down into the river, indicating I should follow. I had not planned on getting wet but follow their example and walked into the river. They walked into the middle where the water came to my chest, which greatly concerned me. I will tell you why later. We continued down the river about three hundred yards and came to a sandbar. They immediately took one of the nets and strung it across what they called a river. We would call it a creek. They indicated I should follow them farther down the river, where they began to teach me how I should drag the net by hooking it on my foot while holding the top part above the water, and the individual on the other side of the river would do the same thing. The ladies would go before us, beating the bushes, running the fish ahead of us. I could feel the fish bumping the net, and I also wondered if there were not other things that might be bumping the net as well. They seem to not have any concerns and were laughing as they watched me in my feeble attempts to follow the example of the individual on the other side of the river and to keep my side up. The farther we got down the river, the harder it became to hold the net, and not only that, I was bogging to the knees in the settlements along the bank, and of course, I also was trying to watch out for anything other than fish that might be lurking close-by. As we neared the other net and began to make a circle, one of the Indian men put on his eye protection and dove down to the bottom of the river and began spearing the fish. As he would throw them up on the bank, the ladies began cleaning them, laughing and having a wonderful time, using a spoon to scrape off the scales. It was an exciting time, and everyone was laughing as though this was the greatest thing in the world. However, as I look back on it, I see one of the greatest times to build the relationship and to let them know I am their friend and I like spending time with them.

Upon our return to their house, I noticed something cooking on the fire. I felt it was probably almost time to depart.

I asked him, "What have you got cooking?"

He replied, "Alligator tail."

"Where did you get the alligator."

The river.

"What river?"

Quickly, he replied, "That river."

I could only look out at the river and think *I just walked up the middle of that river*. My next question was, "Where in the river did you catch this alligator?" Their reply to me was, "A long ways from here." They immediately knew what I was referring to and began laughing, even slapping each other on the back because of this gringo and his fear. He told me it was just a small alligator. I let him know that where there is a small alligator, there is mama and papa. However, it was great fun, and we have a lasting relationship with this wonderful family, who now are Christians and love their newfound faith. They have learned to pray and to participate in worship service, and every time there are activities going on at the church building, this good family is always there. How did all of this come about?

Every time I go to Panama, if I have time, I try to take people to visit this family because of the power they have in changing lives. They do not realize how important they are in the lives of so many. They like to offer what they have. They share their meager food, but the biggest thing they share with us is their love for they have changed us. We all need to realize is not necessarily the big things but the small things that make a difference in the lives of others.

Our group was working from a church building in Santa Fe, Darién, Panama, when it was decided on the last day that we would walk to a community that we felt was not far. If you ask a Panamanian how far it is before we get there or where this community is located, the reply often is "Not far." Most of the time, it's not far, but for us gringos walking, it's far. We left very early in the morning in our vehicles, but after going a short distance, we realized very quickly that this was going to be a walking trip. We park our vehicles alongside the trail, and everyone grabs a box of medicine, their instruments, and their backpacks for a nice little stroll through the jungle, which turned out to be a two-hour walk. Two hours do not sound like much, but if you are a bunch of out of shape gringos, it is a long way. At first, we are following our leader, who knows the way to the community. We are all together, but it's not long until we are all stretched out with some dragging behind because they have to stop and rest. The ones up front do not know this, so they just continue. I am no exception for I am really out of shape.

There were several walking together and did not notice the main body of the group had made a left turn on a small pathway through the jungle. Those lagging behind continued straight on. They said the first sign they were lost was when they ran out of horse poop. I said sarcastically, "I did not know they were following horse poop." We had several people in front riding horses, so they just followed the horse poop. They immediately recognized they were lost probably about the same time we recognized that part of the group was not with us. We sent back some of our in-shape Panamanians to look for them. In the meantime, the lost group backtracked and found where the main body had turned off on a different trail. I asked, "How did you know what trail?" They replied, "We saw some horse poop." I suppose the advice is when you're traveling through the rain forest, watch for the horse poop. As a matter of fact, I suppose we should just put it on the map to follow the horse poop. We learned a very valuable lesson on this day, which is, make sure the entire group all stays together and the one in the lead never forgets the people he's leading.

    I was visiting in the home of some Christians in the town of Santa Fe with my good friend J. W. Furr, someone who had grown to love the people of Panama almost as much as I had. He was always looking forward to the next trip. He decided he would go with me while I was doing some logistical work. We were invited to stay overnight in the home of some local church members, and we gladly accepted their hospitality. It was in the midst of the rainy season, and everything was wet and muddy. None of the houses have indoor toilet facilities, so one must go out the back to the toilet. However, the lady of the house, knowing us gringos, decided she would make it easy on us and got us a can to put in the room where we were sleeping so we would not have to go outside at night to use the toilet. However, my good friend J. W. Furr was sort of embarrassed to use the can. He says, "I don't have a problem going outside to the toilet." He proceeds to get his flashlight and heads out on his mission. Little did he know how fast he would make it to the toilet for when he stepped off the porch, the grass was very slick and traveled downhill. J. W. Furr immediately picked up speed when his feet flew out from under him, sliding all the way to the toilet. It was very close to daylight, and the lady of the house happened to be up. She was getting ready to cook breakfast when she noticed him flying past the window as though he was sliding down a snow-covered hill. I suppose the moral of the story would be, see how fast you can get to the toilet. The lady of the house said she had never seen anything so funny as this gringo sliding down the hill on his backside. I have to admit I have been traveling to Panama a long time and have seen a lot of things but nothing like that.

My two sons, David and Jim, have always loved traveling to Panama with me and have developed a great love for this ministry. We decided to build a house for a family who had recently lost their daughter from a brain tumor. They desperately needed a house to replace the shack they were living in. Getting others to go with us, we made arrangements to build it. There was not enough room for us all to stay in one location; therefore, some would stay with a local preacher and his family. David, Jim, and I will stay with the family who we are building the house for. There was not a lot of room for us all, so David occupied a small single bed while Jim and I slept on a piece of foam rubber on the floor. To be honest with you, I was not too happy about having to sleep on the floor, but this was a mission trip of my own planning, and I had not planned well for our sleeping conditions. Our host family was trying to make us gringos comfortable, so we did not complain because some of them were sleeping on cardboard in a kitchen that had a dirt floor.

It also was very hot, and the mosquitoes were enjoying a nice meal on us. I always wondered why they didn't bite the Panamanians. When I asked them if the mosquitoes were biting them, they replied, "No, not much." We were prepared, however, and proceeded to spray insect repellent very heavily, and now we are lying there, trying to sleep, full of insect repellent, all greased up, sweating for there was no fan. The one good thing was that the mosquitoes were not biting, but we could hear them buzzing around. We finally dozed off, and some time during the night, my son Jim lets out a screech as though he had been attacked by some vicious animal. I asked him what in the world was going on. His reply was, "Something ran across my feet. I believe it was a rat." I am not afraid of a lot of things, but I hate rats. They just give me the creeps, so about now, we have our flashlights turned on, trying to find a rat that had just run across Jim's foot. I shine my light around under the bed and see a pair of eyes looking at me. I jump back and fell over Jim, who was behind me, who in turn fell over David, who was behind him. We started shaking the bed, hoping it would one run out, and it did, right between my legs, back over Jim's foot, and out the door into the other part of the house. However, it was not a rat; it was the family cat that was seeking out its normal place to sleep, which was under the bed. We found this out the next day. Following this, Jim would not get back on the floor and made his brother, David, move over on the single bed. It had been many years since David and Jim slept in the same bed, and neither one was very happy about it. Jim had no intention on getting back on the floor. I started laughing, trying not to wake up everybody else in the house. The next day, when we were describing our events of the night, trying to get the family to understand what was going on, they thought it was the funniest thing that they ever heard. They were not afraid of rats because they have them in their houses. The next morning, as I walked out the door, a large rat ran across the beam, trying to escape. There wasn't much worry on me doing anything to the rat for I am deathly scared of them.

In 2003, we were working in the mountains of western Panama outside the city of Santiago. The president's office had asked us to take our surgical team and work from the Santiago hospital. The general medical group traveled for two hours by several government 4×4s into the mountains that surrounded this province. When we go to these areas, most do not have facilities. When I say facilities, I mean things like bathrooms. This has always been a situation where all of the women would have problems for obvious reasons. Most do not like to go to the bathroom because the outdoor toilets have a very serious odor. Also, we have found varmints inside the toilets. We usually would send some brave Panamanian soul and check it out before any of us gringos would venture inside. I wish I could say that the situation was going to be better just because the secretary of the president of Panama City had arranged for us to go to this community. Some of those government officials were accompanying us as we went from community to community providing health care. The one good thing we had going for us was we were in western Panama, where it was much cooler, and one would not have to drink as much water and therefore not have to go to the bathroom as often. You can almost watch people when they start looking out at the bathroom, which usually was positioned behind the school or building we were using, usually quite a distance out back for obvious reasons. It began to get late in the evening, and time was getting close for us to start loading the trucks for a two-hour drive down the mountains for our return trip to Santiago. A nurse practitioner by the name of Diane Edrington asked one of the assistants, Belinda Tipton, if she had any of the little packets of wipes for none of the bedrooms had toilet paper. She gave her one, and Diane proceeded to the bathroom. No one is paying her any particular interest for everyone is packing and getting ready to go. All of a sudden, we hear a screech, and we all run to the back of the building where the screaming is coming from. Diane is screaming and running from the toilet, pulling her pants up as she comes out the door. "Something bit me on the bottom." One of the Panamanians runs into the toilet to find out what had bitten her. She still had in her hand the paper that the wipe was wrapped in. She looks down and discovers that her very good friend Belinda had given her an alcohol wipe instead of the regular wipe. No one laughed any harder than Diane did after discovering she was not going to die, at least not today, from snakebite. It took a while to get the message over to all the local people who did not understand what the problem was, but when they came to understand it, it was hilarious. I suppose the next time anyone on a mission group will look very closely at what they use for toilet paper.

    I suppose with any mission group, one of the greatest joys we have is to bring people to an understanding of God's will for their them. It has been my privilege to baptize a lot of people in the rivers throughout Panama. Sometimes it is a challenge to find a hole deep enough in order to baptize people, epcially during the rainy season. Therefore, I have had a number of instances that were very humorous. I do not make light of the baptism itself because it is a wonderful experience to be part of someone as they turn to Jesus Christ. On two occasions, some young people expressed an interest to be baptized. They asked if I would perform the baptism, and I was overjoyed to be asked to participate in this very important decision of their life. During the rainy season, we have to be very careful because the rivers are up and they are swift.

    I was baptizing two young ladies late in the evening of February 2012. We all walked about half a mile to the river and found it running very swiftly. I walked out in the water to see how it felt and could feel it tugging at my legs, but it was not so bad that I could not baptize them. One of them had very long hair and was very skinny. She did not seem to be very nervous because most of them grow up around the rivers and are not afraid to swim even in the swift waters. I asked her if she was ready. She said yes and stepped into the water. The water was not terribly deep and only came up to her waist. I was not paying close attention to the direction the water was flowing. I decided to baptize her with her head going downriver. After I talked to her a little, explaining to her exactly what I was going to do, and after a short prayer, I took her down into the water, and immediately after she got under the water, she was jerked out of my hands by the swift waters. I did the only thing I could do and grabbed her hair and held on and pulled her back to me by her hair. I grabbed her arms, pulling her out of the water. She began to laugh, being not bothered nor afraid. Those standing on the bank started singing "I Have Decided to Follow Jesus." It was all I could do to keep from laughing at having to use her hair like a rope to reel her back in. It was time for me to baptize the other young lady. She suggested that her hair was not as long and we needed to find another place that was not so swift. I looked around and found a part of the river that was behind a bend and noticed the water was smooth, so we went over there and baptized her without event.

Another time that we were in the town of Santa Fe, a fairly large man wanted to be baptized. He was not tall but had a big belly. He was smiling and was so happy that he was about to have his sins washed away. A Panamanian preacher who was speaking in this revival was to baptize him. This was during the dry season, so there was not a lot of water in the river. As a matter of fact, parts of the river were dry. Looking down at the river, it was about twenty-five feet from the top of the bank to where the water should be. The preacher began to walk around stepping in different holes hoping to find enough water to totally immerse this man. The man needed to be totally immersed for that's what baptism is. This preacher was up for the task and sits the man down in the water. The man is smiling for he is happy for what is going to happen to him today. Remember, he has a large belly and needs to be totally immersed. A short prayer is said, "I baptize you in the name of the Father and of the Son and of the Holy Spirit. Amen. This gentleman is laid back into this puddle of water, and all of the man is under the water with the exception of about six inches of his belly. The preacher, for some reason, thinks that he can just push the man's belly down as he laid him back, and as he pushed on the man's belly, water shot up about a foot as the air was pushed out of his lungs coming out his mouth and nose. Everybody standing on the bank could not contain themselves, and Cristobal looks up at everybody with a big grin on his face for he cannot contain himself. He brings the man up out of the water, and the man himself began to laugh. He has been born again and he is happy. He was not at all humiliated but took it all in stride and was just happy to have been baptized into Christ.

God is so good to allow us to be part of seeing people turn their lives over to him. It is a wonderful experience, and perhaps the greatest part of mission work is being part of the conversion of people when they make the decision that Christ is going be the center of their lives. This is why as we traveled throughout the rain forest, going into the villages where the indigenous people live and where so many are so hungry for the Good News of Jesus Christ. I have baptized people in holes of water that you would say had an anaconda in them, but in all the places I have been, I have not yet encountered one single problem because when you're doing the Lord's work, I believe with all of my heart that God will make things turn out for good. He has never failed us yet.

SNAKES, CHIGGERS, AND PICKING RICE

I am the world's worst at putting my foot in my mouth. Sometimes when I am with others and I offer for us to help someone, they often reply, "What are we volunteering for?" Of course, all that is said in a joking manner, but sometimes it is true because not only is it out of my comfort zone, it is beyond my ability to perform the task at hand. I've always said that we North Americans have become too soft, which I quickly found out upon my offering to help pick rice. "Have you ever picked rice?" I was asked. I told Manuel Pimentel I had picked corn when I was a boy. I picked peas and butter beans, so how much harder could it be to pick rice?

Another thing that I am deathly scared of is snakes, and snakes are always on my mind when I'm walking through the rain forest or just across some field. I'm constantly looking about, watching where I put my feet. That was a statement from my father many years earlier on the farm. "Son, watch where you put your feet."

I arrived in Torti with my good friend and Christian brother Mike Ray. I found Manuel and his family had gone to the field to pick rice. Upon further inquiry, I found it was not too far away. We only had to cross one ditch and several fields, walking in grass up to our waist, which made it difficult to look out for snakes. We had not been walking long when I commented to Mike that every time I volunteer to go somewhere or visit someone we had to walk in this kind of terrain. Not only were there the snakes to worry about but if you did not spray on insect repellent heavily, you would literally be covered with ticks and red bugs. This is the part of mission work I hate—red bugs or, as some people call them, chiggers. This is a misery you do not want, and I believe every red bug in the world is in Panama. I asked the Panamanians why they did not get red bugs. They simply replied, "Red bugs do not like brown skin." They began laughing at one another at the joke. Manuel replied in his broken English, "Red bug like white skin." Looking around at everybody, he translated what he said, and everybody laughed.

When Mike and I arrived where they were picking rice, we noticed they were making teepees out of the rice or what looked like teepees because it was stacked that way. They all had on large Panama hats to protect them from the hot Panama sun. And believe me, it was beating down. Mike and I were exhausted just from the walk. We watched them pick for a few moments, and I decided I would try to pick some of the rice. I had talked to one of the Peace Corps girls who lived in the mountains. She indicated to me that she picked rice with her host family and said it was not that hard to do when she mastered the little cutter that latched on to your hand. This consisted of no more than a bone that had been sharpened and a piece of leather or string tied to your hand. I watched for a while. They were very fast at cutting the tops off the rice, tying them in bundles, putting them in the basket, which they had on their back. After they had the bundles tied, they would then be stacked in different places throughout the field. Later, all of the rice would be hauled on their backs to their houses, where it would be beaten out and bagged, and then they would take it to a mill.

After, I thought, *I can do this.* I found out very quickly it wasn't as easy as I thought and decided that this is not as easy as picking corn. Mike was not very encouraging to me when he said,

"Larry, I think you need to leave picking the rice to Manuel and his family." I could not disagree with him, and the more I tried, the more they laughed. Manuel said to me, "Brother, we pick rice; you watch. You have rice in United States?" I told him we did have rice but not in Alabama and where they did have it, big machines picked it. He knew all about the big machines because the big companies all around the area had the big machines. We decided we would just stand by, watch, drink our water, watch out for snakes, make sure we had bug spray on us, and give them moral support. The more I participated and try to be a part of their families, the closer we became. They all knew I could not pick rice and did not have the ability to do a lot of the other things they were doing, but they knew, I loved them.

The longer I stayed in the field, talking, laughing, and just being there, I was building a bridge that would span a long time and would have a great impact upon not only their life but mine and Mike's.

I'M NOT DRIVING DOWN THAT CLIFF

I was about to start my twentieth year of mission work in Panama, and little did I know that this year was going to get started off with a bang. I had been approached by Fernando Gracia, minister of health under the Moscoso administration, to travel to western Panama to the town of Santiago and take with us an eye surgery team, general medical, dental teams, and other support personnel. The president's people would decide where we would work in different areas. I learned a lot on this trip about not working with those in politics, but that's not what I want you to see in this part of our story.

    The government of Panama asked us to travel to distant villages and communities located in the mountains surrounding Santiago. Some mornings, we would drive two to three hours through the mountains and arrive at a school or other community building. One morning, we began our drive traveling down a one-lane dirt road, and we approached a very wide river. This was not a small river but at least one hundred yards wide; however, it was not deep as one would think due to the time of the year. The water did come up to the headlights. The river bottom had huge rocks, so there was no danger of getting stuck. There were no bridges, so the drivers had to be skilled in driving this type of terrain. We decided that only two of the nine trucks would cross the river. Our destination was a small secluded community that was seldom visited by any type of medical team.

Diane Edrington and I decided we would stand in the back of the truck so we could see better. We also had the best driver, and when he hit the river, he never let off the gas, and one would've thought we were riding a bucking bull in a rodeo. What fun it was. The second truck was not so lucky and stalled out as soon as it hit the water. So we continued with the one truck. Fortunately for us, all of our medications were in our truck. About three or four hundred yards from the river, we came to what I would call a cliff. It was not straight down but close to it. Riding with us was a liaison from the president's office who had to be crazy in the head. He tells our driver to go ahead and drive on down this cliff. The driver says, "I'm not going to drive down that cliff." The man asks, "Why? Are you afraid?" The driver says, "I'm just not stupid."

We decided to park the truck and walk the rest of the way.

We came across a group of people building a mud hut, which consisted of digging a big hole, putting water in it, and mixing up the mud. They would then put straw in the mud, plastering it on the sticks that have already been put in place. All of those who were in the pit were already about drunk. We learned this was the way they built these mud huts, with everyone working and drinking throughout the day until they were all drunk.

There were quite a few people waiting for our medical personnel to help them with their medical needs. This took a couple of hours. We then hastened to cross the river due to the rising of the water. If we did not hurry, we would be stranded on the opposite side of the river until the next day. We went back to the river and were able to make the crossing without further incident.

Each day, we traveled to different communities throughout the mountains. Some days, we traveled as long as four hours to reach our destination. I was surprised where we found people living and that the government of Panama was aware of the plight of these people, but little was done to help them. They were very sweet people who were desperately poor, broken off from the rest of the world. On our way out of one of the communities that consisted only of families scattered throughout the hills, we stopped on top of one of the mountains for a break. The scene was extraordinarily beautiful. I wondered if the people themselves knew just how beautiful the surroundings were.

On the last day, we were told by the liaison officer we would be traveling to a community about three hours from Santiago. Someone at the hospital asked us where we were going. We told them the name of the town, and some of them started crying. We were to travel by helicopter, but because of some problems on the border to Columbia, the helicopters we were to use went there instead, leaving us the only transportation available—nine four-wheel-drive trucks. Our destination would take us though about ten miles of rain forest. This was the dry season, so we felt we would have no problem with the drive. However, what happens in the rain forest? It rains, not hard, just a fine mist all the time. We finally arrived at the road that enters the rain forest. All the drivers get out and lock in their four-wheel drive. A doctor from Panama City who worked with us all week said to me, "Now the fun begins." We travel for about a mile with no mishaps. The road is very slippery, and one of our trucks slides into the ditch and is almost on its side. Everybody in the truck climbs out the other side. It took us a while to winch the truck back up on the road so we could continue. Once we were traveling again and getting deeper into the rain forest, the roads were getting much worse. Everybody was having a big time or at least almost everybody.

While we were stopped, my wife noticed something sticking out of the vines, which were very thick. She said, "That's a little boy's head sticking out of the tree." Yes, there were children in the trees, watching the gringos invading their territory. I suppose it had been a long time since they had seen this many vehicles in one place especially this deep into the rain forest. We eventually came to a small community on top of a hill. Who would've thought one would find what we found in this area of Panama? It was extraordinarily beautiful with orchids growing around about waterfalls. The people were some of the sweetest we had met and also some of the poorest and most needful.

Everyone pitched in as we began to set up our medical clinic. All the medical professionals immediately began working because we would only be here a few hours. We needed to try to get back on the main highway by dark. Some of the group prepared Vacation Bible School and worked with the children while they were waiting to see the doctors.

Everything was going well until our liaison individual came running up to me, saying, "Larry, we need to get out of here fast." I thought something really bad was happening. The problem was it was getting around four o'clock, and everyone was afraid we would be there after dark. We loaded up all of the trucks as fast as we could and headed out. I was in the last truck for all the others had already left but didn't get very far. I pulled up behind one of the trucks and got out to walk up to the front to find out what was going on. I remembered this long hill as we were coming in but did not give it much thought. I should have for now it was an obstacle, and our first truck was only about halfway up, and he wasn't going anywhere. We all went up the truck to try and push it but to no avail. The truck with the winch should have been the first truck up the mountain, but where was it? It was the last truck, and we could not get it around to get in position to do any good. My wife gets out of the truck she is in and proceeds to walk up to the top of the mountain, as did some of the other ladies. They sat down to watch the show, and what a show it was. We actually were having a good time. I told them that people pay upward of $5,000 for an expedition like this. However, some of those with us did not see the humor in what I had said. I just kept joking and laughing with everybody, trying to make sure no one panicked, because it was getting close to dark, and we did not have one single truck to the top of the hill. It took us at least two hours to get one truck to the top. By midnight, we had four trucks out of nine to the top of the hill. I say to Dr. Alberto Arrocha, a doctor from Panama City, "We need to go with the trucks we have." He agreed, but how do we get people who had come in nine trucks into four? It was really funny to see so many people packed into the trucks. Some of our Panamanian workers stood on the bumpers, and we took off on what turned out to be a fantastic mud ride. The drivers were not planning on getting stuck again. It's what you would call real mud riding. Everybody was having a blast even though we were very, very tired. We still had at least three hours ahead of us. About an hour later, we finally came out on the pavement. We stop the trucks so that the drivers could take off the chains that were on the tires, but due to so much abuse, the chains were almost welded together, and we could not get them off.

While our drivers were beating on the chains, another truck approaches, to our delight. It is what we would call a real 4×4 being high off the ground with huge tires with a large winch on the front. Driving it was the private secretary of the president of Panama City, and with her was the director of the hospital from Santiago. When we had not arrived back by midnight, people became very worried and decided they would come and see if they could find us. We eventually arrived back our hotel in Santiago at around 3:00 a.m. I told everyone that this was a trip for the books. One of our nurse practitioners, Diane Edrington, a very adventurous person, said, "I would not trade it for anything in the world. I loved it!"

The next day, at our devotional, I had people think about the good that was done in the name of Jesus Christ. At no time were we in any physical danger. I thought about the people we had met, especially the children in the trees who were so amazed yet so excited to see us and to receive the treats we gave them. Many people were sick and received medical attention with everyone receiving parasite medication and vitamins. More importantly, they received instructions of God's plan for their lives.

THE CLINIC OF HOPE

One would have to travel throughout the Darién Province as I have to really come to an understanding why I suggested building a clinic in that area. Some had asked me why the Darién and not some other place in Panama. The Darién Province is not where most people who live in Panama City or even in western Panama want to go because they had heard so many bad stories about this beautiful area of Panama. After an individual travels to this province, they then can understand why I love being there so much. Why do I return time and time again to this part of Panama? Not only is it extraordinary in its beauty but also in its inhabitants. It is the home for the Wounaan and Embera people as well as some of the Kuna Indians who live in parts of the Darién on the Caribbean side. There are an estimated twenty-two thousand Embera and seven thousand Wounaan Indians; however, these numbers are dwindling. They still tend to live in thatched-roof, open-sided huts on stilts. The stairway leading up to the living quarters is a log with steps chopped into the side oftentimes made from balsam wood. If the log is inverted, with the notched steps pointing down, it is a sign the family wants privacy. At night, the log is pulled up to keep out unwelcome visitors. Life among these people is relatively simple where the man will burn off a particular spot and plant their crops of corn and other vegetables. After a time, they will move to another location and do the same thing over again. wikipedia.org/wiki/Embera-Wounaan

I first visited this area in the midnineties and found a people that were at large neglected by their government.

I am not criticizing the government of Panama in this book, but as in all third world countries, a large part of the population is neglected and must rely upon groups such as Panama Missions. For many years, I took groups into this area to try to make a difference in the lives of the people such as the Indian population. Some have even suggested that we should not spend our time helping a people who have chosen to live this way. My answer has always been and always will be that these people love their culture as I do mine. I once spoke to one of the chiefs, saying to him, "I did not come to your village to change your culture nor to force you to believe the way I believe. I only want to share my faith and demonstrate the compassion of our Lord Jesus Christ."

Into this area, we come, as have other groups, to strive to make a difference, and we are struck by so many needs, from health care to proper hygiene. Sometimes lifestyles do bring about health issues, and as much as we want to help, we can only do what the people will allow us to do.

Such was the case of two babies by the same mother brought into Alto de la Playon, an Embera community. One baby was about five months old and the other close to two years old. The smaller baby was totally blind while the other child, according to his mother could see if she held the eye lids open. After Dr. Joe Wilhite and Diane Edrington along with other nurses examined these children, it was determined that the baby perhaps did not even have eyeballs. The other child was also examined and perhaps could have surgery to correct the problem. I asked the mother if the children had ever been examined by a doctor, and she replied no. We questioned the chief of the village about the possibility of taking the children to Panama City to the children's hospital. He explained to me that the father would not allow this because the father said the doctors in Panama City would do more harm to the children. This is something I have never understood. The chief said he would not intervene in the lives of a family, and if they chose this, that is the way it would be. When the father finally relented and said the children could go, we made arrangements for the children, but when the time came to travel to the city, he changed his mind. None of us understood this, but we have to live with it and pray for the family.

Some people we found when they have a disease just live with it even though it becomes life threatening. For example, in 2012, Dr. Joe Wilhite and Diane Edrington examined a man with half his face completely eaten away by cancer. Had it been treated properly, he might have lived a longer life. It was a horrible sight, and this man suffered terribly. This is why we decided to build the Clinic of Hope. People, like this man, who had no other place to go could come to our clinic and then we in turn refer them to Panama City, even helping them with transportation and food.

We wanted to make a big difference in the Darién Province, and the question was how we would go about doing that. This was the big question. How do we bring about better health while not infringing upon the cultures of the people? We wanted to bring about hope where there was no hope. Let me give you an illustration of what I am talking about and why we made the decision we did.

While visiting in one of the villages of the Darién, I was asked to visit and pray with someone who was very ill. I climbed up into their house and found a young mother lying in a hammock with a high fever. I put my hand on her forehead, and it was hot to the touch. I am not a doctor and did not pose as one. The mother was so weak and so dehydrated she could hardly speak. There were two problems here. One was she was very sick from some form of a fever, perhaps malaria, unable to eat, and had no medication. The other problem was she had a two-month-old baby, and she could not nurse the child. The child was fast becoming dehydrated from a lack of milk. The first thing I did was have a prayer with the family. I then inquired about taking her to the nearest clinic, of which they said to me, "We went to the clinic, but they had no medication. We were told we could go to the pharmacy and buy some medicine, but we had no money. They told us to go to the store and buy a lot of juice that would help with the dehydration, but we had no money for this either." I made arrangements to immediately purchase formula for the baby, medicine for the mother, and different juices so she would overcome the dehydration.

I realized this was only for the short term. I could help this family overcome this situation and perhaps save the life of this mother and this baby, but what about the future? What about the next time and the next time? I knew that I must make some form of long-range plans in order to help these people. This is when we decided we could not just sit back; therefore, we came up with this idea of building a small clinic in the Darién. For people with more serious illnesses and injuries, we worked with contacts I have made in Panama City in getting them into the hospital or give them whatever care was needed.

One will find small clinics scattered about throughout the Darién Province; however, they are very ill equipped with little to no medicine. The doctors are frustrated and have so little to work with. That is when I came up with the idea to build a small clinic directly on the Pan-American Highway, eighteen miles from its end in the community of Sanson. I did not realize when I made this decision how challenging the next three years would be in its construction. We faced all the challenges from getting materials in to the filing of all the proper papers for becoming a legal clinic.

Working with David Brady, a builder from Birmingham, Alabama; Bill Watts, a retired builder now living in Birmingham,

Alabama; and Allen Gunn, owner of a company that builds portable buildings in Tallassee, Alabama, we, with much prayer and determination, built what we now call the Clinic of Hope.

It stands two floors high surrounded by banana and mango trees and other tropical plants. It is beautifully done and truly has brought hope to many people who live in the Darién Province. People have walked for many hours to have our medical personnel examine them and then issue the proper medications. Travelers along the Pan-American Highway stop and take pictures for they are amazed at this accomplishment. God is good. God is good all the time. We are his servants, and we are happy to serve the people of Darién.

Groups from the United States travel at least three times a year to work out of the Clinic of Hope. The clinic downstairs has a pharmacy, three exam rooms, a dental clinic with two chairs, which allows the dentists to work simultaneously, and a large waiting area. In the next few months, we will install a laboratory.

Yes, it has brought hope to many people of the area and not only hope to have the physical needs cared for but a hope that comes only through the Savior. Through this facility, not only do we give physical counseling and help to the hurting but, for those who desire, we try to improve their spiritual health. No one is turned away because of what they believe religiously or do not believe, but rather, our desire is to help them come to an understanding of God's will for their lives. This is the goal of all mission works throughout the world. The Clinic of Hope offers that hope.

WHAT PLEASES GOD

I believe that any book about mission work would not be complete if there was not some discussion about the importance of pleasing God. I have discussed this issue with others who do mission work in other parts of the world, and we all feel the same way that far too much money is being spent on big expensive church buildings. Most of us who do mission work have something to say about this subject. That is whether we need them or not. It is not my intention to criticize those churches that have such buildings; however, is God pleased with this, and what does it do for the spirituality of people? Over the years, we have helped a number of churches build a meeting house, and they are always proud of having a place out of the elements. It does not have air-conditioning and sometimes does not even have electricity, but they are happy.

One of the first things that hit me when I first began doing mission work was the absence of comfortable places to worship or what I felt was comfortable. I have traveled around the country, speaking about mission work and how to be effective, and one of the things I address is how far we have gone to make our membership comfortable. I wonder if we have not lost some of the spirituality in our mega buildings where millions of dollars are spent for us to worship our God. I believe it brings up a question, and this question has not only been asked by me but has been addressed by others. What pleases God? In order to please

God, must we spend the biggest part of the contributions in order to make the membership comfortable? While we spend our megabucks to make our membership comfortable, there are those who do not even have a place out of the elements to worship. In my search throughout the New Testament, there is no place where this question about buildings is addressed. Therefore, it would be up to the leadership of a particular church as to how much money should be spent on their meeting houses.

In early 2012, I was on a mission trip in the Darién Province in the community of Sanson. There is a church building close to where the Clinic of Hope is located. The church building was in very poor condition, needing a new roof. The entire electrical system was in very poor condition as well. When we have medical teams in the area, we normally have worship at night and work all day, seeing patients. When evening came on the Lord's day, people began to show up for worship. All of a sudden, we lost electricity in the entire community, leaving us in the dark; however, this did not deter the Christians from assembling for worship service. We took all the chairs and put them outside, and people continued to come even though there was no electricity. The crowds continued to grow, and for all of us North Americans, this was a real treat. It wasn't long until a large crowd assembled under the stars for the purpose of worshiping God. I believe with all my heart that God was pleased that night even though we were not inside a beautiful building.

One good brother stood up and began leading singing from the heart without the aid of songbooks. The singing was enthusiastic as they sang song after song. We sang songs in English, and they sang songs in Spanish, and our hearts blended as we worshiped. We did not understand each other's language, but the common bond we had together was tremendous, so we sang a song entitled, "A Common Love." We had much in common for we were all part of God's family even though we were from different parts of the world. We prayed in English, and we prayed in Spanish. A young man by the name of Tito Miranda spoke, doing a tremendous job of encouraging us all. Then we participated in Communion, remembering the death and the suffering of our Lord Jesus Christ. The point I'm making here is simply, I believe God was smiling down upon us. Yes, I believe this is what pleases God.

Several years ago, we began working with the Kuna Indians located in the community of Ipeti. This is a large community of over one thousand people. They have a very special place in the hearts of so many of us. The Kuna, as do many indigenous people, believe in their superstitions and myths, even having their own medicine man and *silahs* (chiefs). Working very diligently and patiently, we were able to convert a number of these sweet people. They began meeting in the house of one of the new Christians. One man in the village who became a Christian said, "We must first work with the children." And so we did, thus began a new church that grew from the children. There was a need now for a meeting house and a discussion again about what they needed. In talking with the church, they decided they needed a small cement-block building located on the reservation close to the road where everyone could see it when they passed by. A minister by the name of Hoyt White from Long Beach, Mississippi, literally fell in love with these people and their simplicity of life. He wanted to take it upon himself to raise the money and build this building. He did not want it to take years to do, but he wanted to go ahead and build the building, and he would take the responsibility of paying for it and raising the money. Finding a local builder who was familiar with this kind of work and with a drawing on a piece of paper, he began working on the small building, and when it was completed, the entire community was elated. They fill the building every Sunday, mostly with children. I know God is so pleased when he hears their voices in the Kuna language praising his name. There was no electricity in the community, so they always worshiped before dark, but it did not dampen their spirits.

Several years after the building was completed in the year 2011, electricity was brought to this community, and we helped them put electricity in the building so they could have lights. No, there's no indoor bathroom or running water or any of the facilities that we hold so dear. Children's classes are held outside under a thatched-roof building with wooden benches. There is no shortage of children who want to be in the class. When we are there conducting Vacation Bible School, we take the children in the large field adjacent to the building in a large circle. They hold hands, sing, and play games. This has changed the lives of many of the young people from the United States.

Yes, they change our lives and help us understand more about what pleases God. It is always said we returned to the United States rejuvenated, ready to be a better member of our congregation. We learn, I believe, more about what pleases God when we assemble in the worship services throughout the world where they do not have all of the luxuries that we so much cherish in our country.

FINDING HAPPINESS

People look for happiness in many places and in many things. We give our children things to make them happy. All seek happiness, but few find real happiness. Why? They look in all the wrong places, in all the wrong things, and oftentimes, with the wrong motive.

We as parents desire for our children to be happy. To fulfill this goal, we begin filling their lives with things. Wow! We get so excited when we see our children happy, when we see them laughing over some new item we have purchased.

Where is true happiness found? This is the twenty-million-dollar question. For one reason or another, people desire to participate in a mission trip. A doctor said to me, "I want to go on a mission trip and don't even know why." Perhaps, he, like so many, was seeking to fill a void in his life. Perhaps he had friends who had been on mission trips and, upon their return, saw something different about them. Maybe he wanted to go for this is where he was to find happiness. Perhaps it was to find contentment.

Still others go because they said this was their calling from God. For whatever reason people go, they are influenced in ways they never believed possible. Their lives are changed forever. The change makes them better parents, better children, and better leaders at church and in their community. Perhaps even more important, they have become better servants. I believe that in all of this, they found the happiness they were looking for but not in the ways they thought it would come.

There were no riches, nothing one can buy to cause what happened to them possible. How is it I feel different, they say. A doctor who had been traveling to Panama for over thirty years on mission trips said to me, "Why do I keep on returning? I have to say, it is the people." Isn't that amazing for one to get so touched and so moved that it changes him or her as a person. The giving of oneself could be the! void they felt was missing. The question is, what was it about the mission trip that brought about this discovery? Of all people who participate in mission trips, 99.99 percent find happiness that leads to contentment. This discovery is not temporary. They return home to find themselves not being able to forget what has happened, the things they saw and the people they met. They just cannot get these things off their minds. Why? One Christian lady said, "It was truly a *National Geographic* moment." She never had seen nor participated in anything like that. The videos she had watched and the pictures she had viewed did not prepare her for the things as they unfolded before her very eyes. The poverty, their needs were so great, leaving one feeling that one has to do something to make a difference, that one cannot just sit by and do nothing. She said, "It overwhelms you. It controls you. The void you have felt, the true happiness you have been seeking unfolds as you begin to plan."

I wrote about Peter earlier in this book and how we saw him running and limping up to the group. The thing that touched the group was how Peter laughed and joined in with the fun and games. All of a sudden, Peter is on everyone's mind. What can be done for Peter? There are so many Peters around the world. We all need to find a Peter because this is where true happiness is found. Just like the man already mentioned in this book who went around looking for another little boy who had lost a dollar, so often, people come to me, having been touched by a child or a situation, looking for ways to make a difference in the child's life. They return home, and unlike so many experiences, the past two weeks will not leave their thoughts. They tell the story over and over again and even make albums to show their friends and family. Everybody wants to hear about the trip. They want to know why you are so excited and why the difference. All of a sudden, plans are being made for the next trip.

Yes, I believe this is true happiness when a person gives of themselves and separating themselves from all the things that at one time made them happy. So many have found that something that has been lacking in their lives. They begin collecting items for Operation Christmas Joy or medicines for the medical team and items for Vacation Bible School and so many other areas of participation.

The following stories are written by people who traveled to Panama and now admit their lives are different. Each one has related to me how they found true happiness.

HOW MISSION WORK CHANGED OUR LIVES

PANAMA FIRE EXPERIENCE
JESSE STANFILL

I am a twenty-four-year-old intensive care unit registered nurse from Lexington, Tennessee. I had the opportunity to go on my first medical mission trip on February of 2011 to the country of Panama. Having a weakness for anything adventurous, of course I accepted, and it changed my life. There were sixteen of us, a mixture of doctors, nurses, dentists, and ministers. We even found a couple of Peace Corps workers that joined us in the rain forest. The sight I saw after stepping out of a dugout on the banks of the Chucunaque River was comparable to a page in *National Geographic*. The lush plant life and exotic animals were enough to make me stand in awe. Then I met the people: the Embera and Wounaan tribes. Most did not even speak Spanish but spoke their own language. They met us on the beach with big smiles on their faces, so at even thousands of miles away from my house, I felt at home. The people of Panama, especially in the Darién area, had suffered a massive destructive flood the December before we arrived. Those people touched me in ways I did not expect. They had lost their homes, possessions, family members—everything.

Our presence was big news. Most had never seen a doctor or nurse before, let alone a blond-haired, blue-eyed girl like me. I had ibuprofen and Tylenol, pure gold to them! I saw sickness and disease running rampant, even leprosy. In the midst of treating their ailments, I kept yearning for more—more education, more knowledge, more supplies, and above all, I wished I could help them more. The second day in the village, we ran out of children's antibiotics. We had more at the mission, which was a thirty-minute boat ride and forty-five-minute bus ride away; it was completely out of my reach. Tears filled my eyes as I scanned the crowd of villagers that had gathered. My eyes rested on the children. I had to walk away. "Get a grip," I told myself. "Don't cry." I pulled myself together and went back. No one was turned away; we treated them all with what supplies were left. I saw in their eyes that they had hope. Seeing Jesus work through us, Christians, gave them that. At the end of the day, yes, I was tired, but something had happened, not in a physical way but a spiritual way. I felt a fire burning inside me. The feeling was penetrating my external layer, piercing through my soul, and encompassing my spirit. I was saved as a young girl. I grew up in church with my family. So I thought, is it possible that I am saved again? I thought I already had my salvation. I came to the conclusion that this was my "burning bush" experience. I am not saying I spoke to the Lord like Moses. I am saying that the Lord was so present on that bank of the Chucunaque River in Panama that I could feel his fire. It felt good. In fact, good does not describe it. It felt amazing, marvelous, tremendous, and absolutely wonderful. My fire was fed repeatedly the rest of the trip. My heart was touched by every little child with a stuffy nose and every patient's joyful Upon returning home to Tennessee, I found myself seeking the Lord. I wanted him in a way I had never before. I wanted him to continue to use me in any way possible. I did not want to lose my Panama fire. I soon realized the obvious: that Jesus is working not just in Panama but also right here in my community. Why had I never seen this before? My eyes were reopened in Panama. This led to my volunteering at the Regional Inter-Faith Association. At first, I just organized donations. Then I came across a project called Snack Packs. Food packs for children of unfortunate families are assembled weekly for them to take home and eat over the weekend. Before Snack Packs was started, these children would go home on Friday after school and not receive another meal until they returned to school on Monday. A school nurse in our area saw this need, and thus, Snack Packs was born. A nurse just like me did this great thing. How inspiring! This is Jesus at work.

Jesus presents himself so often in our lives. He gives you opportunity after opportunity to witness him and to witness to other people for him. One incident I experienced after that first trip to Panama was with one of my patients. I will call her Lucy. Lucy was in her sixties and diagnosed with pneumonia a few weeks earlier. Following a bronchoscopy, she obtained a new diagnosis—pulmonary fibrosis. Her lungs were getting hard like stone. This made it impossible for her to oxygenate her body. As time would go on, her lungs would keep getting hard until eventually, she would suffocate. It was a Friday, and the doctor told her that she would probably not make it through the weekend. She needed to make any plans and say her good-byes to her loved ones. This was, of course, hard news. I held her hand while she took it all in. The doctor left the room; her husband, John, followed him to ask a few more questions. Lucy looked up at me with tear-filled eyes. She had a hard time speaking due to the BIPAP machine she was wearing to help her breathe. Again, I felt that fire, my Panama fire. I asked, "Lucy, are you a Christian?" She gave a muffled yes. She stopped crying and put her hands out to me and bowed her head. Our thoughts were one. I knelt down beside her and prayed as hard as I have ever prayed before. I asked her if she would like me to call the minister. She then asked me a question I did not see coming. She asked, "Does he perform marriages?" I know I looked confused because I definitely was. I asked Lucy why she was asking me this, and she responded, "John and I never really got married, and I want to marry that man before I die." I thought to myself, how am I going to do this on a Friday afternoon? I did not want to get her hopes up, so I told her I would just look into it. I walked out of her room and was told that John had gone home to change clothes. My Panama fire was burning intensely by this point. I immediately called their daughter and explained what Lucy had just requested on her deathbed. I could hear her daughter start to sob on the other end of the phone. I told her I would call the county clerk's office, but she would have to get there before they closed to pick up the paperwork. She agreed and would also inform her father. I began enlisting my coworkers to help me. It was already four o'clock in the afternoon, and we had to work fast. The hospital minister agreed to stay past his shift to perform the ceremony, the secretary was arranging a wedding cake and sparkling cider to be sent up, and my director bought a wedding gift for the couple. We even had the hospital notary on standby to make the documents official. When John and their daughter arrived at five o'clock, marriage documents in hand, we were ready. Lucy had no idea what had taken place just for her. John walked in first while all of the nurses were peeking through the cracked door. You can only imagine the overwhelming emotion we felt when John dropped down on one knee and proposed to his true love. As soon as we heard her say yes, we filed in with the minister for a quick ceremony. There was not a dry eye in the room, especially when the minister replaced the words "Till death do you part" with "Forever and always." Lucy was a married woman, and she was finally at peace. She moved out of the ICU, and I visited her every chance I got. In my visits with her, she never seemed troubled again. In fact, she took great pride in sharing her story. She would even show anyone who came by her wedding pictures, which I had taken with a disposable camera. She passed away almost two weeks later. The hospital thought the story deserved recognition, and it received the Hearts Afire Award for that month—an incentive program for employees who go above the job for patients and families. The hospital gave me fifty dollars for doing what I did for Lucy, and I thought to myself, I did not do this for money. This was Jesus at work. So I did what I thought was most fitting. I gave the fifty dollars to Larry, founder of Panama Missions. My eyes were open to Lucy's spiritual needs because of Jesus being in my heart and in that room with us. I know fifty dollars do not seem like a lot of money to us here, but on my second mission to Panama, Larry put the money toward buying the buckets used for the water filters that were given to the people. These families in Panama now can drink clean water, which is better than any medicine. What better way to spend fifty dollars? I can't think of one.

My experiences in Panama reopened my mind, body, and soul to the Lord. We don't always realize what we need. Sometimes we think we need that new car or we need that special someone to love us. Most of the time, we need a void in our life filled. Jesus is the answer. I have found nothing is more satisfying for my soul than the work I do for him. Put your trust and faith in the Lord. Maybe you have already done that. Maybe you just need a spark to start your fire again. I find myself praying for other people to have the "Panama fire" experience. I will continue to pray for that, for you.

AUTHOR'S NOTE

Jessie has now been on her third trip to Panama and has entered nurse practitioner school at the University of Tennessee so she can better equip herself in helping others. She has been such a blessing to all of us and a great inspiration to everyone who she comes in contact with.

MY EYES WERE OPENED
CATHERINE SALES

The Panama Mission trip I was fortunate enough to go on was an unforgettable, indescribable, monumental moment in my life. I had prayed and prayed for God to present an opportunity for me to serve and begged my mom to allow it. God was so gracious. He presented my family with this opportunity, and we took it. I went into Panama not knowing what to expect, and what I learned and felt from the experience was definitely bigger and better than I had ever anticipated. We visited two villages, both very different.

The first village we reached by a hollowed-out canoe. Upon arriving at the village, the children and people of this village greeted us anxiously. I was taken aback. The sight was one you never see in real life. It was like we had stepped into another world. The village was brightly colored, but the extreme poverty was undeniable. We set up a place to treat patients in the middle of the village. As soon as we were ready, the people swarmed in. I got the chance to work with patients, taking blood pressure, handing out eyeglasses, and other small tasks. That was not what I ended up doing though. The children took away my attention. They clung to me and another girl, Ragan, who is close to my age. They treated us like we were angels. They loved us unconditionally even though it was our first time to meet. This really hit me.

Maybe God was trying to show me something through these sweet children. Although they lived in conditions nightmarish to anyone in America, they knew something Americans did not—how to love someone regardless of race or background. God was trying to show me that this is what he called us to do—love as these children did.

While in this first village, there was one man whose story must be told. This man came into the clinic limping, supported by a walking stick. Translators explained to us that he had traveled days to find us and get medical care. Both of his feet were broken and had been this way for years. How was this even possible? This man was the true embodiment of God's power and strength. He had walked farther than most people back home would in their lives and did this with both broken feet and without complaining.

Also, everyone in the village had stomach worms from drinking the unclean water. God is all-powerful and almighty, showing himself in many ways throughout this trip but also showing the group that we must appreciate what we have and give thanks to him. He truly reminded me how blessed yet unworthy I am throughout the trip.

Our journey continued at the next village we visited. This village was culturally different than the previous village, but we saw the same type of impoverished people and harsh living conditions. We found people literally living on top of each other and had contracted diseases from this kind of lifestyle. The village had a culture ran by tradition. The women had to marry at a young age, cut their hair, and wear a certain type of dress. It made me realize how lucky I am to have freedom and identity as a girl in America. We met a girl around my age who spoke a small amount of English. She took us around the village, showing us how these people live. When we came to her house, she presented us with a gift. She had nothing, yet she was giving us a present. She showed us complete selflessness. It was astonishing and touching.

The most memorable moment of the trip for me was an unexpected one. It was the last day for clinic, and I was just cleaning small wounds and things like that when a hysterically crying baby was brought in. Ragan and I were put in charge of taking care of this baby because the others were so busy. The baby was struggling to breathe and had an unnaturally high temperature that could do extreme damage to the baby's brain. It just hit me at that moment that the baby's life was in our hands. I had never seen life like this, and how easily it can vanish. The whole time we were taking care of the baby, a constant prayer was replaying in my head. God was with us in that moment more than I had ever felt him.

God truly blessed me on this trip. Although I was sent to help others, I ended up gaining so much more than I could ever have given these people. They taught me more than I ever imagined possible about selflessness, worship, appreciation, and so much more. These people really showed me how you can have nothing, but if you have God, you have more than you could ever need. Possessions loose value, and the truth is exposed. God is all we need; the people of Panama taught me that.

THERE SHOULD BE NO EXCUSES
AMANDA WILBURN

Mommas are busy people. Pharmacists are busy people too. Christians should be busy people. I happen to be all of those things. An average weekday for me goes a little something like this: I wake up at 5:00 a.m. and exercise. I make the coffee and savor a cup on the back porch. I choose clothes for myself and my six-year-old based on which ones are the least wrinkled. I put them in the dryer to "iron." I take a shower and get dressed for work. I awaken my six-year-old, Eli, and sweetly ask him to hurry and get ready for school. I awaken Cory, my husband. I tell

Eli to hurry again. I pack our lunches and sign the homework folder because I forgot last night. I tell Eli to hurry! I brush Eli's hair and teeth because I am in a hurry and he is not. I make the chocolate milk and grab a couple of breakfast bars for us to eat in the car on the way to school. I drop Eli off at school and go to work at the pharmacy. I take phone calls from health care providers, verify prescriptions, and review medication profiles to ensure there are no drug interactions or intolerable side effects. I compound specialty drugs including suppositories, capsules, creams, and lollipops that are otherwise unavailable. Around 2:00 p.m., I realize I'm hungry because I forgot to eat lunch. I stand at the pharmacy counter and choke down a sandwich between phone calls. I have to rush because a newly diagnosed diabetes patient and his parents are coming in this afternoon for an insulin pump consult. My shift ends at 5:00 p.m. today, but I have too many loose ends to tie up, so I stay until 5:30 p.m. I leave and drive to the soccer field. Luckily, Cory got off work in time to pick Eli up at the after-school babysitter and help him change into his uniform. The game is entertaining and lasts an hour. No one has had supper, so we stop at the sandwich shop for a quick healthyish meal. We get home ten minutes before Eli's bedtime. I run his bathwater while Cory helps him with his homework. Eli takes a bath. He wants to read me a bedtime story, so we choose a book. I tell Eli good night. On the way out of his bedroom, I grab his hamper and head to the laundry room. I start a load of laundry, and then I wipe down the kitchen counters. There are many more chores that need to be done, but my legs are aching, so it will wait. I turn on the computer and check my e-mail. My eyes are heavy, but I haven't completed my Bible lesson today, so I open my Bible and start to read. The next thing I know, the alarm clock is buzzing, and it is time to start all over.

I love my crazy, hectic life. My son and my husband mean the world to me. Our extended family is very close, and we spend as much time as possible together on the weekends. My grandmother has had some health problems recently, and I want spend time with her as well. Friends are important. Bible study is important. Work is important. I volunteer for a local charitable organization, and that is important. Cory and I are trying to adopt our second child, and that is important (and very time consuming). My church family is important. Cory and I both teach Bible classes, and that is important. Sometimes I feel my faith wavers because there are so many important things that I need to take care of and there is no way for me to do them all effectively and well.

I have two younger brothers, Joshua and Caleb. The three of us are as different as night and day, but we all strive to serve others. I love them both dearly. While in college, I went on a mission to Argentina to help host a Bible study camp. Josh was a Bible student at the time, and I talked him into going with my friends and me on the mission trip. I assisted with collating Bible study materials, cleaning the camp, and teaching women's Bible classes. I came home from the first mission and went on with life. I started my pharmacy career. Cory started a new job. We bought our first house. We had our miracle baby, Eli. I began working part-time and stayed home as much as possible. Eli is in kindergarten this year.

One day, I was talking to Josh on the phone, and we were reminiscing about the first mission we completed together. That first mission trip was life changing for me, but I told him that I felt like my talents could be used to a greater degree on a medical mission. He told me about Ms. Beverly, a nurse who worships in his congregation who is part of a medical mission team to Panama.

The next Sunday afternoon, Cory, Eli, and I were spending the day with my parents. My cell rang, and I was surprised to learn the caller was Ms. Beverly. She told me the Panama team could use a pharmacist, but if I wanted to go, I would have to book my flight immediately because they already had tickets. She also said the deadline was approaching to send in our medical licenses and visas in order to receive permission from the Ministry of Health to work in Panama. The left side of my brain immediately came up with numerous excuses to stop me from going. My thoughts were as follows: I could not leave my family. Eli was too young. I had too much responsibility at home. How would Eli get to school? Would he cry every day? Was I being selfish even thinking I could leave my little family for ten long days? What if something happened to me while I was gone? Could they make it without me? Cory doesn't usually pay bills or grocery shop or take Eli to school. He wouldn't want me to go. Worse still, what if something happened to Eli or Cory and I couldn't get home to them? What if the adoption agency calls while I am out of the country? There is no way I can afford to book a flight so soon. I needed more time to plan. It would be too difficult to go on a medical mission at this point in my life. Maybe someday in the future I could go, but not now. It just was not possible.

Next, God showed me that I was not in control. We went back to worship that very night, and Cory mentioned to the church leaders that I had been invited to go on a medical mission to Panama. The church offered to purchase my plane ticket. I felt like that was my way of knowing that God wanted me to go and he was going to take care of me. I booked the flight the very next day.

On the Friday morning that I left for Panama, my youngest brother, Caleb, took Eli to school. As I walked out the door, Eli smiled and gave me the biggest hug ever. We said our goodbyes and I love you's. Eli didn't cry at all. I didn't cry either (sort of). On Saturday, we arrived at the Clinic of Hope in Sanson. People were lined up outside the building, waiting for the team to start clinic. We dropped our suitcases on the floor and got to work. I've never worked so hard in my life! On Sunday, we set up in the clinic again. That night, we worshipped together with our brothers and sisters in Sanson. On Monday, we packed up the pharmacy and traveled out into the native Embera villages. That night, my body was tired, but I couldn't sleep. My life was forever changed. My roommates were sleeping, and I didn't want to bother them, so I pulled out my cell phone and tapped out my thoughts. Let me share those thoughts with you.

IF YOU HAVE SHOES ON YOUR FEET

> Again I tell you, it is easier for a camel to go through the eye of a needle than for a rich person to enter the kingdom of God.
>
> Matthew 19:24

Today, we woke up early and had grits for breakfast (grits brought with us from the States). We loaded onto a bus and drove through the rain forest for about thirty minutes. When the road ran out, we hiked down a hill to the Chucunaque riverbank. We got into a canoe or dugout made from a hollowed log and sat on milk crates. Two young boys maneuvered the canoes while another used an old juice carton to dip water out of the canoe and back into the dirty river. We rode for one hour and finally reached the Embera village. Many children along with the chief of the tribe met us at the riverbank in excitement. We unloaded our supplies and hiked up into the village school to set up our clinic. People lined up to wait their turn to see the health professionals. We had translators converting our English into Spanish and the native Embera language. I had shoes on my feet. They did not.

During my time in the Darién Province, I was technologically cut off from the world. My cell phone didn't work. The iPad was at home. There was no Internet service. There was no TV or radio. The only thing there was God's beautiful creation. I felt very close to the Lord. I had shoes on my feet. They did not.

There was a hostile protest against the Panamanian government by the Embera and Kuna Indian tribes, but I felt at peace. I was miles away from my family, but I felt at peace. I was exhausted, but I felt at peace. There was nothing to distract me from my reason from being on this earth. I was able to worship with brothers and sisters who looked nothing like me. My skin is light; theirs is dark. My hair is blond; theirs is black. My eyes are blue; theirs are brown. I am tall; they are short. We were dressed differently. I had shoes on my feet. They did not.

We sang simultaneously in three different languages, and it was beautiful. The surroundings and the love shared between Christians made me feel like God gave me a little glimpse of what heaven will be like, except maybe we will all have shoes on our feet.

We are very much an overindulged society. We have so much to be thankful for. If you have a headache, you can go into any pharmacy at any time and buy ibuprofen for four dollars. The Embera waited in line for hours just to get one bag of pain reliever. Many of them would then send their children through line or get in line again themselves and hope we didn't recognize them just to get a second bag. There is no money. There is no pharmacy. There is no car. There is no road. Many of them will not receive another bag of medicine until the mission team goes back next year. When those people see that bag of four-dollar ibuprofen, they see Jesus. What do you think about when you see ibuprofen? What do you think about when you put your shoes on your feet?

Tonight, I lie on a thin foam mattress in Sanson. I had beans and rice for supper. I took a cold shower under a PVC pipe. I am sharing a bedroom with six people. My shoes are stowed safely under the bed. I am a rich woman.

Again I tell you, it is easier for a camel to go through the eye of a needle than for Amanda Wilburn to enter the kingdom of

God. Now, if you have shoes on your feet, replace my name with yours and let us remember to be humble and gracious always.

AUTHOR'S NOTE

Amanda made her first trip to Panama in 2011 and was immediately hooked and is preparing for another trip taking her husband and other members of her congregation where she worships. She helped organize the pharmacy in the Clinic of Hope and has grown to love this mission. She plans on making many trips in the future. Her and her husband live in Corinth, Mississippi.

PANAMA AND ME
REBECCA HARRIS

My first trip to Panama was in the year 2005. I then traveled with Panama Missions on a mission trip every year after that. On my first trip, we went to the town of La Palma, the capital of the Darién Province. Located on the bank of the Atlantic Ocean was a prison unlike anything I had ever witnessed. They were very receptive to the Gospel and seemed to enjoy the time we shared together. I have been advised that they were living under some very harsh conditions with some of them not having proper beds. This was probably the reason so many of them were suffering from back pain.

We also worked out of one of the local schools, seeing hundreds of patients who, although were so poor, seemed to be happy. After I returned home, I had so much more appreciation for my faith for everyday comforts, like a bed, food, shelter, a real hamburger, and a cold Diet Coke. Another thing that I found such a great appreciation for was the availability and easy access

To Change a Life

to medical care. I learned that even though there was a language barrier, the smile was universal.

Part of our medical mission in 2005 was in an Embera Indian community. There was so much about this culture I did not understand. Girls marrying so young was one of my greatest concerns, and this kind of lifestyle saddened me deeply. I was also deeply saddened and started crying one day when we had so many children and not enough medicine or not the right kind of medicine. Our group leader Larry Brady, told me that I needed to remember the words of Jesus when he said, "If all you have is a cup of cold water and you give it in my name you will not lose your reward." I heard Larry, but honestly, I think it had taken a few years to be able to accept it in my heart.

There were other missionary doctors and nurses and helpers I have had the honor of serving with—Dr. Joe Wilhite, a retired surgeon; Diane Edrington, a nurse; Jerry Ervin, an EMT; Belinda Tipton, a teaching assistant; and so many others that have touched my life by their service and their love for others. They have been a great example of compassion, endurance, love, and generosity. One morning, as we were eating breakfast, another missionary lady from Mississippi by the name of Shae showed me an example of service and humility. The Panamanian waitress served her meal, but this wonderful lady decided to make sure the children who were not even part of our group were served first, and then she received her meal last. You might say she was a real kid magnet and was a joy to be around.

I also noticed how hard the local Panamanian ministers worked, perhaps the hardest working men I have ever seen. They preached and served the church while still working their farms and taking care of their families on a small income. When the Panamanians sing, their whole heart is in it, praising God to the highest.

I noticed very quickly that Larry thinks and eight-passenger van will hold twenty people, and sometimes it does. Coming down from the mountain one night from worship, a family of five rode with us to an intersection of dirt roads. They had arrived early in the day to receive medical care and stayed for worship. They were smiling and waving good-bye to us. That is when I found out they had walked almost three hours one way that day. Wow, I should never complain about a twenty-minute car ride to church with air-conditioning and comfortable pews and lights in our church building.

I found the ladies of the church in Panama to be extremely hospitable for they would rise early in the morning and stay up late to prepare and serve our meals. Once when we spent some time with our Kuna brothers and sisters I thought it was the coolest thing when I was able to help them prepare food for our group. I helped Vail peal potatoes and carrots and cook over an open fire. During our spare time we found that sports was universal when some of our group began to interact with the young people doing situps and push-ups and laughing and congratulating one another.

One of the highlights of my journeys to Panama are church services in four languages—Kuna, Spanish, Embera, and English. A little old lady not much over four feet tall came into the clinic barely able to walk, and there was very little we could do for her; however, we gave her a used walking cane that was adjustable to her size, and she began to cry after receiving this gift. She had the worst curvature of her spine I had ever seen and still was able to walk. She told me that no one had ever shown her this much kindness. I told her that Jesus loved her very much and so did we. There was a man who we named Snake Man who had been bitten by a very poisonous snake thirty years earlier, and the wound had never healed. We could literally see the bone, and he had it wrapped up in an old rag. As I cleaned and washed his wound laughing and joking with him I was over joyed when he later turned his life over to Jesus being immersed having been forgiven of his sins. The

Peace Corps who served as our translators were remarkable young people who lived under such dreadful conditions.

I suppose one of the greatest impacts upon my life is the day my two sons, Paul and Thomas, traveled to Panama and served in ways they never thought possible. They worked every day, mixing concrete on the ground, pouring a floor for a local Christian family who had a mud floor. I watched them holding babies, which was so unlike Paul yet he seemed to love it so much. It changed their lives, making them better servants. Our daily devotional singing with fellow missionaries was a highlight of our day when we could praise God and thank him for allowing us to serve and be part of this group. The cold showers were just part of a mission and did take some getting used to. In 2011, the nightly devotionals were led by Caleb Cochran and translated by Maranda Jennings. The devotional was about what it meant to live as a Christian and how these young people had the same problems as North American teens deal with.

There was always some type of adventure in our travels, coming to Panama or on the return trip. We had forgotten luggage and medical supplies, were stranded in Miami for seventeen hours. When we were returning home on Interstate 85 while waiting hours for traffic to clear after an accident, we had Communion and a worship service in the middle of the highway. One of the most intriguing things that happened in my travels was the time when we missed our flight in Atlanta. Joy and Jerry Galloway from Geneva, Alabama, were with me. The flight to Panama from Atlanta is three hours and forty-five minutes—but not on this day. We were routed on another airline to Los Angeles, California, a four-hour flight, transferred to another airplane for another four-hour flight to Panama, and arrived very early in the morning, exhausted. Jerry Galloway, a dentist, demonstrated to me great humor and love with his joking around and acting so crazy, all the time. I fell in love with Victor one of our translators who was so humble and sweet and dedicated to this ministry. Victor passed away in 2009. Yes, so many memories with so many lessons taught to me about how to be a servant and what it really means to serve. I am truly a better person for having learned to be what God wants me to be.

AUTHOR'S NOTE

Rebecca Harris is n registered nurse who lives outside of Montgomery, Alabama. She works as an emergency room nurse and has traveled to Panama on numerous medical missions, using her talents in service to others. Her abilities and her smiles have touched us all and has made her a favorite; they have not gone unnoticed by the doctors and even all the local people. She is always gathering medical supplies and trying to determine what else we need to complete the mission. She has been an asset to our medical teams and is loved by all. In 2011, she took her two sons, Paul and Thomas, to help with construction projects such as pouring concrete floors. Paul attends Auburn University in Montgomery, Alabama, and Thomas attends Hooper Academy.

WHAT TOUCHED ME
JOE WILHITE

The year was 2000. At the age of seventy-one, a retired thoracic surgeon, I made my first mission trip to the Republic of Panama. I was working as a physician in an emergency room in Lexington, Tennessee. I do not know what I expected and really did not know how to prepare working in such third world conditions. I was introduced to a very different kind of medicine that I have been practicing in the United States. Many of the diseases I saw in Panama were diseases that had been related to me in medical school many years ago. The people had many medical problems secondary to the mosquito such as denque fever and malaria. I have never seen a case of leprosy, but on this mission trip, I saw leprosy as well as many other tropical diseases I had only read about it medical books.

As I began seeing patients every day, finding them to be very patient while waiting for hours in line with hope in their eyes, I found them to be very generous with their love and appreciation of our efforts to help them. To show their thankfulness, oftentimes they would return with gifts they had made themselves such as baskets, jewelry, and pots. One optometrist that was working with us received a chicken. The people would give us what little they had. I suppose the best example of their appreciation came to me when I was called to see an elderly gentleman who lived in one of the Kuna Indian villages. They live in huts next to the river and sleep in hammocks. They also drank water from the river as well. The elderly gentleman had a very bad urinary tract obstruction that required an instrumentation to relieve his bladder. It required more than one trip, and on my last visit to him, he and his family had prepared a hammock for me in their hut and invited me to stay with them. It was the only way they could show their appreciation for what we had done for him.

In the year 2012, we were working in an Embera Indian community a short distance up a river. There were many people who lined up to see us, and I really thought in the years I had traveled to Panama, I had seen just about everything until a middle-aged man came into the clinic with half his face gone from perhaps some type of melanoma. I really do not know what kind of cancer he had, but it had destroyed his face. As a medical doctor, we are there to help, but in this case, there was nothing that could be done. I found this man to be very humble. Perhaps he felt he only had a short time to live. I know that the people come to us Americans for they really think we have the medicine to fix just about any problem.

We have searched and continue to look for other things to relieve human suffering in this small part of the world, and it came in a very inexpensive way with a small instrument one can hold in their hand as it changed the lives of the people who live in the Darien province of Panama. This was in the form of a small water-filtration system to clean even the dirtiest of water for the people were having to drink the dirty water from the river. This is the same river where they bathe and wash their clothes. This little filter will improve their health considerably 365 days a year. It will promote healthy children and adults with fewer diseases such as malnutrition and gastroenteritis.

Yes, Panama Missions has renewed my medical knowledge in tropical diseases and made me appreciate the need for mission involvement. It has made me appreciate the gentle, loving attitude of the poor of Panama and the enjoyment they give me. But the greatest thing that has happened to me is how it expanded my faith in God. I am now eighty-two years old and plan on continuing this mission work as long as my health will allow me. It is my plan to become more involved in helping others have a better day.

AUTHOR'S NOTE

Dr. Joe Wilhite along with his wife, Millie, have made many trips to Panama to serve people there. Dr. Wilhite is a retired surgeon who now lives in Lexington, Tennessee. At the age of 82 he is not ready to stop for he is a doctor full of compassion and loves the people of Panama. He is always trying to think of other ways he can help the people. We are greatly indebted to his leadership, his compassion, and his encouragement to the rest of us.

TEARS OF JOY
RUSS BURCHAM

For the past twelve years, I've been blessed to experience many tears of joy—tears of celebration and praise to God—when people who have been blind for years receive the miracle of vision in the name of Jesus.

When the eye patch comes off after cataract surgery, the joy is incredible. I've heard an elderly man who was blind from cataracts for seven years tell his wife, "I'd forgotten how beautiful you were!" I've watched a forty-eight-year-old mother look down at her two-year-old baby and see her smiling face for the first time.

I've seen the joy in the face of a sixty-year-old woman who, for the first time in years, is now able to see well enough to weave a basket and help with simple family chores.

As we watched these events, we all cried tears of joy as each person gave glory to God for their life-changing gift, saying, "Thanks be to God."

These experiences are common on the mission field, where people are out of their comfort zone, serving and teaching, not knowing what the next day will hold for them. When we give up our life in service to him, he gives us life-changing experiences.

Yes, it required some sacrifice on my part and sacrifice on the part of all who chose to help in the mission effort, but we know that God always pours out his blessings on all those who "die to themselves, take up their cross, and follow him." The small sacrifice of time, money, and effort is quickly overwhelmed by joy and blessing.

I personally have been able to experience (for a moment) what Jesus must have experienced when he healed the sick and gave sight to the blind. When we become Jesus to this lost and dying world, we become God's ambassadors, sharing hope and love to helpless masses of people. There is no other experience that can bring such tears of joy.

Through these efforts, I become more like him, and my faith grows. I know that many are brought closer to him, his kingdom grows, God is glorified, and Satan is defeated. The end result is that I get to experience life the way God intended. Why wouldn't I keep coming back for more?

My hope and prayer is that each person reading this will take the step of faith needed to have these same experiences and that you would be changed and blessed through tears of joy.

AUTHOR'S NOTE

Dr. Russ Burcham along with his wife, Vicki, live in Denver, Colorado. God sends people in many different ways to participate in mission trips. I received a call from Dr. Burcham over thirteen years ago, saying he would like to give back what God had given him in the form of a talent to make people see. Over the past thirteen years, he along with other ophthalmologists have restored the sight to over two thousand people. This is something money cannot buy. Dr. Burcham said to me, "I just want to use my talents to help others."

IF NO ONE KNOWS I EXIST, THEN NO ONE KNOWS I LIVE
DIANE EDRINGTON

Each time I give a presentation on medical mission work or tropical medicine, I start out with this quote: "If no one knows I exist, then no one knows I live." Over the years, I have been blessed to travel to many foreign fields to practice health care to those who would otherwise have none. I never before knew that certain people existed, whether indigenous tribes of Central and South America, nomads of the Sahara, or villagers along the Nile

River. I now know of their existence and their lives. As I traveled among people less fortunate than myself, it has changed my life forever. It also has challenged me to give back what I have so richly been blessed with. So this is where my story begins.

In the year 2000, I was asked to be a part of a medical team supported by Panama Missions to go to Panama and provide health care to a community on the Caribbean. My friend Paula asked to go along and assist in any way needed. We were to meet a medical team from Colorado for instructions as this was our first mission experience. We arrived in the community of Miramar and quickly set up medicines and equipment we had brought. To our dismay, the Colorado team had been delayed three days due to flight changes, but the people of the community were unaware and showed up for clinic. Several hundred people lined up outside our clinic at 7:00 a.m. as Paula and I looked at each other overwhelmed, not knowing what to say, as there were only two of us and hundreds of them. This is what we came for, and we began seeing patients with a multitude of medical problems, from gangrene, infections, hypertension, Diabetes, epilepsy, and malnutrition among other medical problems. As night approached, we could not believe the number of people we had helped and how tired we were but how overwhelmed with what had taken place. Our adrenaline was running as we tried to rest for the night when a knock on the door came at 3:00 a.m. A frantic mother brought her three-month-old child having febrile seizures. "Please help my baby," she screamed. Paula quickly took the child as I grabbed necessary medications. The outcome was good, and the mother thanked us over and over for saving her baby. I told her, "God saved your baby, and we were only servants sent to help you and your baby." *Servant*—that word has forever been the force that changed my life and continues to take me again and again into the mission field.

Over the years, treating patients and seeing conditions I did not readily recognize caused concern. In a particular case of a rash that continued to worsen, I was later to learn that it was leprosy. I was treating something I knew nothing about, and I became so concerned. If I did not know what I was treating, then what good was I, and how could I help these people? You see, I was comparing certain medical conditions to those I see in the States, and it was totally different. These were tropical diseases, and I was determined to learn how to identify and treat such diseases. In 2009, I was accepted into the Gorgas Institute of Tropical Medicine and Infectious Disease in Lima, Peru. There I experienced an intense study, working among the experts and learning tropical diseases and treatment, graduating on the Amazon River with such excitement knowing that now I could be of help to the people I served in Panama.

Through the years, Panama Mission built a clinic deep in the rain forest in the Darién Province serving over thirty-five thousand indigenous tribal people as well as rural Panamanians. We now are able to offer general health care, dentistry, and this year, we started a woman's wellness clinic, offering pap tests, prenatal and postnatal counseling among other female health concerns. We also continue our trips upriver, setting up clinics to provide health care. One tribal chief came up to me and, through interpreters, said, "What an honor to have this medical team in our village. You are the first to come help us, and we have so many sick people, especially children. They drink the river water and become sick. Please do not forget us and come back." You see, I know they exist, and now I know they live. "We will be back," I told the chief, and promises are kept as we plan a medical trip there in June 2012.

Every year, millions around the world die from waterborne diseases. How to bring clean water to these indigenous people has been a concern for Panama Missions. Raising money always hampers a dream, but determination usually finds a way. Members of Panama Missions are raising money through churches, service organizations, and personal donations to purchase water filters. This project is beginning to see success as people are learning how clean water can improve their lives and prevent disease. Living in the United States, we think nothing of turning on the faucet and drinking clean water without fear of disease. Luxuries such as flushing a toilet as water returns to fill the bowl or taking a shower as clean water warm rushes over our body do not exist in the mission field.

    I guess you might say it had me when I first looked out and saw hundreds of people gathering to be seen, and I have never been the same. I thank God every day for making me a servant not only for the people of Panama but for those in my clinic at home. People are the same everywhere except some have access to health care and never have to worry if medicines will be available or if their child will lose their life because no one was there or if the contaminated water they are drinking will cause a life-threatening disease. The most amazing feeling I have had as a health care provider is to walk into an exam room in my private office or walk into a hut somewhere off the map and have a patient jump up and hug me and say "Thank you for making me feel better. I was sick, and now I am well." I know at that moment what God has had in plan for me all along.

    Last year, my family and I were invited to witness the final launch of STS-133, the *Discovery* flight. Over the years, I was privileged to witness this amazing event, but the final flight was special. As weather would prevail over technology, the dates were changed, and I was to be in Panama on a medical trip. On a hot, humid afternoon, I stood on the Chucunaque River, teaching a group of indigenous people how to filter dirty river water into clean drinking water. I glanced down at my watch and realized that one of the greatest technological events of mankind was taking place. The countdown had begun, and *Discovery*, with all her might, was thrusting six souls into space to gather information to increase the technology and quality of our lives. There I stood with a water filter in my hand as eyes watched in anticipation of seeing and drinking clean water for the first time. I could not think but how ironic that one great event was taking place at Kennedy Space Center so was another great event taking place on a river deep in the rain forest that most people have never heard of or let alone knew existed. Our team was there, and life changed again for many people. Clean water—now that is a technological event. Today, many people have water filters and are experiencing the results of better health.

Being a part of Panama Missions and serving others has truly been a blessing in my life. I thank God for making me a servant, for wherever I am, I find contentment for helping others has helped me much more.

Now that I know they exist, I know they live, and I pray that God will give me the strength, the health, and the ambition to allow me to continue to be a servant.

For so many years we have shared some great moments in the Panama Mission work. We have shed tears of sorrow and joy, dealt with frustration, and laughed until it hurt, but overall, it has been the best years of my life, and I would not trade one moment that we have shared. Serving those less fortunate through Panama Missions is a gift, and I have been blessed to receive it. I am so thankful for having the opportunity to be part of a lifetime commitment. I cannot forget the time we were stranded in the mountains during a heavy rain, and nighttime came, and we sat in the darkness, laughing about how many people pay thousands of dollars for an experience like this. Then, coming down the mountain, we broke the world record on how many can fit into a pickup truck. Yes, this has truly been the best time of my life.

AUTHOR'S NOTE

Diane Edrington is a certified family nurse in Long Beach, Mississippi, practicing in an internal medicine clinic. She has been involved with Panama Missions for twelve years and continues to make three to four trips a year. Her husband, Max, is an optometrist and is also involved with Panama Missions, providing visual care. Her late father, Hoyt White, spent many years in mission work in Panama and built a church for the Ipeti Kuna village.

MY TROPICAL VACATION IN PARADISE WITH LARRY BRADY

JOY GALLOWAY

In the fall of 1995, Larry Brady came to our office to discuss the possibility of my husband and I traveling with him on the first medical mission trip of Panama Missions. My husband, Jerry, is a dentist, and I am a registered nurse in Geneva, Alabama. He handed us a fancy brochure of a very nice hotel in downtown Panama for he promised us a tropical vacation in paradise. Since we are more of the Motel 6 type, and Holiday Inn is considered extravagance for us, we remember asking Larry a question: "Now how long are we going to stay in this hotel?" For some reason, he smiled and never answered the question. Jerry had already been on a medical mission trip to some remote areas of Honduras in 1987, so he was well aware of what this vacation might be like. Well, we did stay in this hotel for a few hours after arriving late that night. We got up very early in the morning and began our trip to the jungle.

We looked up the definition of a few of the words he used, and *Webster's Dictionary* says this:

vacation—A period of rest and freedom from work own any activity, a time of recreation

paradise—Any place of great beauty and perfection on any place or condition of great satisfaction, happiness or delight

We are still trying to figure out how the words above fit in with the term *medical mission trip*, but we honestly are thankful for the opportunity given to us to work with Panama Missions. What we experienced truly changed our hearts and our lives. It has been our honor to watch so many of these precious people rise above their poverty to know the riches of God's love and grace. We have often said that as we look into the eyes of the patients we are working with, we feel the eyes of Jesus looking back at us.

THE GREATEST BLESSING ANYONE COULD HAVE

MIKE RAY

The combination of medical aid and evangelistic teaching is very effective. When one goes into mission work, he or she gets to do the Lord's work all day every day, just like the apostles in the first century. What greater thing could ever happen to anyone? To see the smiles of joy when the blind is helped to see or the deaf helped to hear or the lame helped to walk or the hungry fed makes you feel like you are living in the first century with Jesus. What greater joy could you have? However, the greatest joy of all is seeing the lost saved. The people are so ready to hear the Gospel, and they are so happy when they come up out of the baptismal waters. It is such a great blessing to see people obey the gospel and turn their lives over to Jesus so that they may gain a home in heaven. I will never forget the visits in the homes and the children we have seen. Some of the things that brought us such great joy were the powwows for the day, the boat rides, and good food. What a great way to end the day. We have enjoyed every minute of it.

SEE YOU LATER
ALLEN GUNN

I was invited to travel to Panama by my good friend Bill Watts to help construct a medical clinic in the Darién Province. The building had been constructed in my company in Tallahassee, Alabama. It was of metal construction and needed someone who knew how to put it together. We all met up in Atlanta, and I was introduced to the leader of the group, Larry Brady, who some jokingly had nicknamed See You Later Larry. I had planned on six days to erect the building but found out I would only have four because of the one-day travel in and one-day travel out of the Darién Province. The first thing this engineer did was take a measuring tape out and check the slab dimensions. At first I thought some Chinese manufacturer had shortened my measuring tape. But I discovered the slab was two feet short. We just made the building two feet shorter. But then there was the stairwell, which was two feet bigger than specified, and the foundation around the stairwell was lower than the slab, and the slab was about a foot too wide. So I wanted to say, "See you later, Larry."

However, I knew to expect surprises, so Bill and I began to develop solutions to the surprises one by one, and before long, the building was going up. Everyone jumped in to help erect the building. Much of the erection of the building required close coordination, and we gave instructions in English and in Spanish. Even though most of us had never met and about half spoke one language and the other half another language, we instantly bonded as brothers with a common cause. Despite the obstacles,

God was with us, and the two-thousand-square-foot building was completed in an unbelievable four days.

Of course, the hotel accommodations were minimal at best, but that's what we expected. We did have soft beds and an air conditioner but no hot water. It was always nice to have a good cold shower after a twelve-hour workday in tropical heat. The church ladies always had a wonderful breakfast prepared when we arrived at the site, and See You Later made sure that we had Panamanian coffee to drink. The same ladies prepared a delightful meal with fresh fruit straight from the vine for lunch. At dinner, we went to a small restaurant in the little town that we stayed in, and the menu was always the same—rice and chicken, rice and pork chop, whole fried fish with eyes and all.

The highlight of the trip was worship with the Panamanians. The singing was beautiful even though I understood very few words. Larry preached with a translator, delivering a very motivational lesson. When offering time came, I could not help but think that most of us have more in our wallet than the average Panamanian who lives in the Darién Province makes in a month. To whom much is given, much is expected. Most of the Panamanian kids sat next to an American and looked up at us with a warm smile. The block building with a tin roof had open spaces in the block walls for windows and open still frames for doors and only a bare concrete floor. The people were all so friendly and appreciative for what we were doing for them and for their community.

Even though I missed my wife while away, when the time came to leave, it was a sad moment. The leaders of the church gave each of us a gift as a symbol of their appreciation for our work. Hopefully, our efforts in a small way will help bring about a better life to those who live there. More importantly, I believe the people of Panama saw the love of Jesus through our actions. For us, we saw people that have little in the way of material things yet seem so content and happy. Seeing their smiles is proof that money and things are not necessary ingredients for happiness. I can truly say it was a life-changing experience, and I am thankful for my good friend Bill Watts, who invited me to go on this mission trip.

LOOKING FOR NEW EXPERIENCE
MARK WHITE

In July 2001, I went on my first trip to Panama, looking for a new experience. I did not know what to expect or where I would fit in on a medical mission. I tagged along with Max and Diane Edrington, brother-in-law and my sister. As soon as I arrived, Larry Brady put me to work, driving one of the two vehicles as we traveled to Colón, Miramar. I was quickly indoctrinated by being stopped by the police as I followed in hot pursuit of Larry's lead vehicle. That was my first trip and was only the start of so many amazing times in Panama. I am not sure what events would have occupied the last eight years of my life. I cannot imagine that anything would have been as rewarding as the work in Panama. Just as one rock thrown into a pond causes a ripple effect in the water, the life of one individual can cause a ripple in the lives of so many others. I am so thankful for having the opportunity to establish an educational program so that many children will be able to have an education. Yes, I would have to say this mission work has changed my life and made me a better person.

AUTHOR'S NOTE

Mark White is a member of the Tennessee District 83 House of Representatives and is the founder and director of the Children's Global Education Foundation.

DOING SOMETHING WORTHWHILE
DUKE JENNINGS

When I left for my first Panama medical mission, I thought I would put in my time and later feel I had done something worthwhile, that I had done my duty, so to speak. I might be able to think I had helped some that were really in need. I was surprised to find other rewards and some changes in my thinking. I discovered that working side by side with my wife/best friend with the sweet people of Panama is really satisfying and just plain fun. What a surprise to find it is so much more than just taking care of a sense of duty to go and do mission work.

It is more like finding what I am actually built for, like finding that a life of service is not a chore, not a grind, but that it is actually a very pleasant and energizing way to live.

Another real plus is to be able to bring good changes in the lives of coworkers that are invited to go on these missions with us. It makes me smile to watch as others discover too that this is a happy way to live and that obeying God's command for us to be servants is, of all things, fun!

AUTHOR'S NOTE

Dr. Duke Jennings and his wife, Sanet, live in Jonesboro, Arkansas. Dr. Jennings is the medical director for Panama Missions and has made several trips to Panama.

MY FIRST TRIP TO THE DARIÉN
FRED HUGGINS

In the Spring of 2011, I was part of a medical mission team that Larry Brady led into the Darién Province. We held clinics at two Indian Villages, treating mainly family-practice-type problems.

As an anesthesiologist, I was somewhat out of my element, but fortunately, I had good colleagues to back me up. It was a remarkable week. The experience made a lifelong impression on me, and I am looking forward to a return trip with many of the same team members. It will be good to see the smiling faces of the children in the clinics as they rummage through my desk, looking for candy. I can't wait to see the beautiful dresses and pride of the Kuna women. It will be rewarding to see the Indians greeting us from the riverbanks. But what changed me the most? It's hard to say. I know that I often think back on the enthusiasm with which they served us meals, and they gave the best they had. Their happiness, in spite of their meager and even primitive living conditions, was a humbling for me. Many of the everyday comforts that I take for granted would be totally foreign to them. Most of the people we met had never traveled more than a few miles from their village. Yet they seemed very content and even very proud and eager to show us their homes. You can't experience these things without being changed by them.

WHAT CHANGED MY LIFE
CAILON STEWARD

When I was fifteen years old, I made the decision to go on a mission trip to the country of Panama. I chose to go to Panama because my friends in the youth group were going, and I thought that the trip would be fun. Unbeknownst to me, this decision to go on this trip would change my life forever. I had wanted to go on this trip for a while because I had seen many pictures throughout my church, and it looked like an exciting experience. We had to work hard from August to June for this trip. We would help prepare and serve at our monthly Panama meals, and we would work the concession stand during the little league baseball games. All of the proceeds were divided by who was working, and it went toward paying off our trip.

While on the mission trip to Panama, we taught VBS to underprivileged children in the community of Las Garzas. Also, we had a construction team and a medical team who provided their services to whoever needed them. This trip humbled my heart and showed me how wealthy I am just to have the simplest of things. We saw where they lived, which were one-room tin or cinder-block houses with tin roofs or whatever they could find. This trip continually affects me today because every year since 2010, I have participated, and every year it teaches me a new lesson. The children are so grateful just to get attention from us, and they really show me how much I take for granted.

In five, ten, or even fifty years from now, I hope to still be doing mission work to wherever God needs me to be. I also hope that I learn a new lesson every trip. My wish is that my family, whether it be a husband or my mom and dad, would still be going and that they would get just as much out of it that I have. I pray that one day my children, grandchildren, and great-grandchildren will do mission work and learn many life lessons. I hope to always be humbled and to never take anything for granted in life. Mission work is a great life lesson, and I hope that in my future years, I will always remember the lessons that God and the children from Panama have taught me.

AUTHOR'S NOTE

Cailon Steward is seventeen years old and lives in Senatobia, Mississippi. She has made her third mission trip to the Republic of Panama. She attends a private school in Senatobia.

THREADING A MACHINE NEEDLE AT NINETY-FOUR
PAULINE VAN HOOSER

I am the oldest woman in our small group of "working for the Master" women.

I was ninety-four years of age when I sewed one hundred dresses for the little girls in Panama. This is when a special relationship began with Panama, God, and I. I used fabric given me by women who did not sew. An ugly material became a lovely dress as I sat praying to God to help me thread my machine needle. It was then I began talking to God as one person talks to another. I built a relationship with God, who always listens, always has time for my needs. I prayed for wisdom to teach the Sunday and Wednesday classes of grandmothers. I saw God's answer in the shining eyes of the women. Many of the lesson taught to me by my parents I relived. How wonderful they were. I altered patterns to make styles Mother made for me. I remembered things long stored in my memory. I know how a little girl felt when wearing a new flippy circle skirt sewn by me as I meditated on my wonderful life. Sewing one hundred dresses has brought me closer to God, to precious memories of my whole life, and to little girls wearing new dresses to worship their God, your God, and my God.

THE JOY OF FULFILLING GOD'S COMMANDS
FRAN ALLISON

Five years ago, we of the Egypt Church of Christ learned about the work of Panama Missions. We are a very small congregation of less than thirty, but we were determined to do all we could to contribute to both their physical and spiritual needs. In the first year, we as Christian women sewed three hundred dresses for little girls, packed shoe boxes for children, collected items for families including sewing machines and other essentials. Our ladies have visited other churches and shared with them the joy of fulfilling God's commands to help one another (Galatians 6:10). We as Christian women have developed a bond of strength and love as we work together to share in their physical needs and to bring them the message of salvation through Christ. We have raised money for Bibles, songbooks, and literature in Spanish along with mechanical and carpentry tools. In the process, we have received the blessings gained by the fellowship of Christian women working together fulfilling God's commands.

THE END OF THE ROAD

The Pan-American Highway runs from Alaska entering Mexico from Brownsville, Texas, to the town of Yavisa, Panama. This segment of the road begins at this point in Panama City but picks up again in Columbia and on down to Argentina, making the Pan-American Highway the longest road on record according to *Guinness Book of World Records*. I have taken groups who have stood at the very end of the road. We then walk several hundred yards down to the edge of the Chucunaque River. The Tuira River runs into the Chucunaque River not far from Yavisa. It took many years before I ventured this far into the Darién Province and I am glad I did for this is the beginning of the Darién gap. One can stand here in this town and see the mountains that make up the national park. Darién is a province in Panama whose capital city is La Palma. Traveling west from Metetí for about fifteen miles, you will come to (the port of) Puerto Quimba. Taking a boat, you cross the bay and come to the town of La Palma. I traveled here many times, bringing with me groups to work at the prison that is located in this town as well as medical attention for those who live here. The Darién covers an area of 4,593.3 square miles. It is located at the eastern end of the country and bordered to the north by the province of Panamá and the region of Kuna Yala. To the south, it is bordered by the Pacific Ocean and then Colombia. To the east, it borders Colombia; to the west, it borders the Pacific Ocean and the province of Panama. In 2010, I traveled down these rivers, coming close to the frontier of Colombia. The one thing that amazed me and also saddened me was the devastation of deforestation. Monster trees have been harvested from the Darién jungles to line the pockets of greedy people. The people that are hurt the most are the indigenous people who live within this forest. The Embera, Wounaan, and Kuna Indians have been driven from their natural habitat. (Exerts taken from http://en.wikipedia.org) I have had the joy and the honor to walk the pathways and ride the rivers in a piragua, which is the typical boat of the Embera throughout the Darién Province. For many years, people asked me to visit this area. I held out as long as I could, and finally, in 1994, I made my first trip into the Darién and fell in love with a gentle and sweet people. I learned what I had been hearing was not true. Yes, one needed to be careful where they went, but as long as we exercised the proper caution, the experience always turned out to be worth the 150-mile dirt-road ride each time. I have wondered why people are so greedy and never satisfied until they destroy the lives of others, and that is what I found because the big farmers turn to burning the fields, making way for cattle and for rice crops and so many other things, pushing aside those who lived there. Rich people came in and begin buying the land from the poor, and having never had this much money, it wasn't long until the money was gone and so was the way of life. They now have to work on the same land they at one time owned simply to feed their families. Life in the Darién is simply about getting to eat today without worrying about food for tomorrow. The people are now having to learn a new way of life that is so different from how it once was. Groups like ours will come and offer free medical care and oftentimes supply them with food and ways to purify their water. Everything I have written in this book is true, and the people that have traveled with me have tried to make a difference in the lives of people who have been forgotten. It is my opinion they are the forgotten people. They are my second family, and as I traveled to the communities, they are always glad to see me. In 2010, we carried Christmas gifts to children who live in this province. This was the first Christmas gift most of these children had ever received. As I stood in the midst of the town of El Real surrounded by children, I had to stop and thank God for letting me come and, for just a short time, interact with them. The small things of life we so much take for granted, a glass of clean water, steak and potatoes. I began to look at my riches and wondered why I had so much and they had so little. I do not question the power of God, but why, God, are you so good to us and they have so little? I know it's this way all over the world with over seven billion people and billions affected by poverty. God has put you and me here to serve, to share, to make a difference. Until every individual becomes aware of their circumstances, that God has put your riches in your hands for safekeeping and we have more than we deserve, do you not think we should share?

The Darién Province is not alone in their poverty, but it's the part of the world I know and have decided to try to make a difference in. Traveling from Sanson to Yavisa and on down to El Real to Pinagama and farther down the river to Boca de Cupe and many other towns, I find myself heavy at heart because I am not able to help everybody who needs it. When one is helped, there are ten more that need help, but because we do not have the resources, we have to pick and choose.

It is my prayer, as you read this book, the stories of real people living real lives and about the people who went there to make a difference, that you to will find a ministry and begin making a difference in the lives of others. What a joy it will bring to you when you find that which has been missing from your life. Do not be like the nine lepers who were blessed beyond comprehension and never looked back to see where it all came from nor were they ready to share the blessing God gave them. Let us not be like the rich young ruler who was so wrapped up in his own life he never had time for anyone else.

Let me conclude this book with the story from Luke 12. It was not until I read this story many times that I really found the true meaning, and it made an impact on my life, and I hope it will have an impact on your life. I am sure you have read this story many times, but let me put it in the form of a story that unfolds on the canvas of an artist. He picks up his paintbrush and perhaps should look something like this when finished.

It might have been something like a big farm somewhere out West. I paint a picture of this man standing, overlooking his vast estate. He's sitting on a beautiful white horse with his beautiful mansion in the forefront. His big barns with the massive silos are not far from the mansion. He is so proud as he looks at all the cows as they graze the rolling hills. We see the beautiful fields of corn growing and blowing in the breeze. It's almost harvest time. He takes off his hat and wipes his brow, and he says to his wife, who is standing beside his horse, "Look at all I have gained. Aren't the crops I planted so beautiful? Yes, I will say to my soul, 'Look at what you have gained. I do not have enough barns to store my goods. I will tear down my old barns and build bigger barns,' and I will say to myself, 'Take thine ease eat, drink and be merry for you have much goods laid up for many years" (Luke 12:19, ASV). I sign the picture "A successful man." God takes the paintbrush from my hand and writes "A fool!"

The man was a fool because he never learned to share. He never said to his wife, "Let's help the family down the road that is struggling. Let's take them some groceries and help them for we have more than we need. God has blessed us."

We always say this man had an "I" problem. Do you have an "I" problem? You can make a difference in the lives of someone somewhere, and if you are a Christian, it is expected.

CONCLUSION

Have I answered the question as to why I went into mission work? I consider mission work far more than just trying to get people to believe the way I do religiously. Perhaps that's why so many people go into mission work, to get others to believe the way they do. I'm not saying this is not my purpose for I believe we must get people to follow Jesus Christ and turn their life over to him as they are immersed into Christ. We believe this is what the Bible teaches, and we should get as many people as we can to follow the Scriptures completely. We all need to set the proper example so others may see Jesus Christ in our lives for this is the message of this book. Have you ever been down on your luck? I mean, you didn't know where your next meal would come from and sometimes you had to ask someone for help.

As you have read throughout this book about the life-changing experiences of different people both in Panama and the United States, you have learned how people did what they did and why they did it. I heard a story one time that really affected me. When we have compassion on others who might be down on their luck the outcome of their life could turn out much differently. What would he have done and what would he have become had not someone intervened in his life? The following story is powerful and I would like to share it with you, the reader, as we close out this book.

"One day, a poor boy who was selling goods from door-to-door to pay his way through school found he had only one thin dime left, and he was hungry. He decided he would ask for a meal at the next house. However, he lost his nerve when a lovely young woman opened the door. Instead of a meal, he asked for a drink of water. She thought he looked hungry, so she brought him a large glass of milk. He drank it so slowly and then asked, "How much do I owe you?" She replied, "You don't owe me anything. Mother has taught us never to accept pay for a kindness."

He said, "Then I thank you from my heart." As Howard Kelly left that house, he not only felt stronger physically but his faith in God and man was strong also. He had been ready to give up and quit.

Many years later, that same young woman became critically ill. The local doctors were baffled. They finally sent her to the big city, where they called in specialists to study her rare disease.

Dr. Howard Kelly was called in for the consultation. When he heard the name of the town she came from, a strange light filled his eyes. Immediately, he rose and went down the hall of the hospital to her room. Dressed in his doctor's gown, he went in to see her. He recognized her at once. He went back to the consultation room determined to do his best to save her life. From that day, he gave special attention to her case. After a long struggle, the battle was won.

Dr. Kelly requested the business office to pass the final bill to him for approval. He looked at it then wrote something on the edge, and the bill was sent to her room. She feared to open it for she was sure it would take the rest of her life to pay for it all. Finally, she looked, and something caught her attention on the side of the bill. She read these words "Paid in full with one glass of milk." It was signed by Dr. Howard Kelly.

Tears of joy flooded her eyes as her happy heart prayed: "Thank you, God, that your love has spread broad through human hearts and hands."

There's a saying that goes something like this: "Bread cast on the waters comes back to you. The good deed you do today may benefit you or someone you love at the least expected time. If you never see the deed again, at least you will have made the world a better place. And after all, isn't that what life is all about?" From An unknown author (http://inspire21.com/)

God's love is shown across this planet through human hearts and hands. I am sure beyond a shadow of a doubt that people who touch the lives of others oftentimes never expected to have the kind of ending that came about. Over and over I have seen people reach out and touch other lives simply because that was the right thing to do at that particular moment. As I introduced this book, you will remember I said people help other people sometimes because it is simply the right thing to do. I am happy to have been part of helping many people find a ministry. When I first began this ministry in 1984, I did not expect the outcome that has affected thousands of lives. I only wanted to help the few poor people I met at church in Panama City. Never did I plan for this ministry to grow the way it did. However, I know that God had a greater plan, and his plan is always the right one. Not only did God want me to bring as many people to salvation as possible but he wanted me to demonstrate his love and compassion to as many people as I could during the course of this ministry. This has happened to the hearts of hundreds of people who decided to travel to Panama with me on mission trips. As you read this book, perhaps you have not found your ministry, but having read what others have done and how their lives were affected, you too can be moved to start a ministry wherever you live in the world. Remember this one thing—you do not have to be a rich person nor do you need to be extremely educated; you only need a heart of a servant. Remember the stories of all the lives that were touched over the past thirty years. Remember those who have received their sight, those that were sick and could not hear, and above all, remember the many hundreds of people that have found Jesus Christ. Perhaps they knew only of you, but they did not truly know Jesus as their Savior. One of the greatest parts of my life was to see people turn their life over to Jesus and allow him to be the Lord of their life.

To be a representative of Jesus Christ throughout the world—no greater opportunity has been afforded mankind. For people to see Jesus in our lives is so vital, and the best way to do that is to follow his example. For each one of you who has read this book, may it be in you to follow the example set before us over two thousand years ago through the person of Jesus Christ, our Lord and our Savior. You can be a soldier for Jesus Christ.

I AM A SOLDIER

I am a soldier in the army of my God. The Lord Jesus Christ is my commanding officer. The Holy Bible is my code of conduct.

Faith, prayer, and the Word are my weapons of warfare. I have been taught by the Holy Spirit, trained by experience, tried by adversity, and tested by fire. I am a volunteer in this army, and I am enlisted for eternity.

I will either retire in this army at the end of time, or die in it; but I will not get out, sell out, be talked out, or pushed out. I am faithful, reliable, capable, and dependable. If my God needs me, I am there. If He needs me to teach a class, to teach my neighbor, to help someone in need, or just to sit and learn, He can use me because I am there! I am a soldier. I am not a baby. I do not need to be pampered, petted, primed up, pumped up, picked up, or pepped up.

I am a soldier. No one has to call me, remind me, write me, visit me, entice me, or lure me. I am not a wimp. I am in place, saluting my King, obeying His orders, praising His name, and building His kingdom. No one has to send me flowers, gifts, food, cards, candy, or give me handouts. I do not need to be cuddled, cradled, cared for, or catered to.

I am committed. I cannot have my feelings hurt bad enough to turn me around. I cannot be discouraged enough to turn me aside. I cannot lose enough to cause me to quit. When Jesus called me into this army, I had nothing materially. If I end up with nothing, I will still come out ahead. I will win spiritually. My God has supplied my needs, and will continue to supply all of my needs.

I am more than a conqueror. I will always triumph. I can do all things through Christ. Devils cannot defeat me. People cannot disillusion me. Weather cannot weary me. Sickness cannot stop me. Battles cannot beat me. Money cannot buy me. Governments cannot silence me, and hell cannot handle me, because I'm safe in my Savior.

I am a soldier. Even death cannot destroy me. For when my commander calls me from this battlefield, He will promote me, and then allow me to rule with Him. I am a soldier in the army, and I'm marching, claiming victory. I will not give up. I will not turn around. I am a soldier, and I am heaven bound, and here I stand! Will you stand with me as a good soldier of Jesus Christ?

Anonymous
(http://home.comcast.net/~davidriggs01/fightgoo.htm)

IN MEMORY OF SHARON EDWARDS

There have been many people who have traveled with me to Panama, but few have made an impact upon me and others as has Sharon Edwards. When it was first suggested that Sharon from Long Beach, Mississippi, participate in a mission trip, I was not for it because of the affliction she had. One of our rules was that people must be in good enough health to endure the difficulties that might come with traveling into a third world country and more importantly on a mission trip, things such as walking long distances oftentimes in very hot and humid conditions. Sharon had polio and wore braces on her legs and at times had to use a wheelchair. I was soon to learn not to be too quick to judge people. Looks are deceiving for Sharon proved to be one of the greatest assets a mission group could want. She did not see herself as disabled. She just could not move as fast as some others could. Regardless of how difficult the trip, Sharon wanted to participate.

She considered herself part of the team and did not want any favors. She worked in the pharmacy and was one of the most efficient workers to ever work in this part of the mission. If someone suggested she sit down and rest, she would always say, "I'm all right. When I get tired, I will rest." She never complained. She taught each one of us so much as we watched her work. The Panamanians also took notice and commented on Sharon's zeal for what she was doing and the love she had for others. She was always smiling and laughing as she worked. All loved Sharon. She has been an example for us all.

Sharon is nearing the end of her battle with cancer. I wanted to see her so badly when I realized also how very sick she was, but she wanted to see me, so I traveled to Long Beach to visit with her in her home. These are her own words:

> I want you to know, Larry, traveling to Panama was the highlight of my life. I was able to go on six mission trips that changed my life for I saw people who were much worse off than me. I learned to be content with what I have and also in dealing with everyday living. Some of the things I thought were problems were actually just bumps in the road for others, I found others have greater reasons to be mad at life than I have. God blessed me more than I deserve. Thank you for letting me go with you to Panama. Please tell everyone there I love them and miss traveling there.

We laughed about some of the things that happened when she had very little to laugh about. I did not want to tire her, so I decided it was time to go, so as our visit was drawing to a close, Sharon said, "Larry, I have no regrets. God has been good to me. I do not question why I got sick and why I cannot live longer. God holds the answers to these questions. I am thankful he has given me these opportunities." I sat on the side of her bed with my arm around her, and we prayed together. I thanked God for letting her be part of my life and so many others and for his will to be done in her life. As I prepared for my departure, I said, "Sharon, if I do not see you again, I will see you in heaven." She replied, "You can know it."

> Sharon Edwards passed away quietly in her home on September 5, 2012. She lived in Long Beach, Mississippi, and was a longtime member of the Cleveland Avenue Church of Christ.